CONTENTS

ACKNOWLEDGMENTS

"Gratitude is the fairest blossom, which springs from the soul."

—Henry W. Beecher

I dedicate this book to my grandmother and aunt, and to all the amazing souls I have had the privilege and blessing to guide on their healing journeys.

I want to extend my heartfelt appreciation to the unseen energies that continue to assist me on my spiritual path. Words cannot express my gratitude to the divine love, which led me to the completion of this book and continues to guide me through my meditations and along my spiritual path.

To all my clients and to Cynthia Thaik, thank you for your love and support.

To Helen Chang, Kristine Serio, Julia Watson-Foster, and the rest of the amazing editorial team at Author Bridge Media, thank you for your heartfelt guidance and expertise in helping me bring this book into the world.

I also want to thank my wonderful husband, Eddie, and our children, Mary and Erik, for all their love and support. You believed in me even when I didn't believe in myself. I love you all with all my heart.

FOREWORD

I am so fortunate to have had cancer. Yes, I said it! Why? Well, this life altering event provided me with the option to change my perspective on life, to challenge my belief system, and meet and work with Kristine. Prior to hearing the words that I had stage 3 esophageal cancer, I was working 60+ hours a week, getting home past 8pm every night to make dinner for myself and 2 children, then eating late and heavy, just to get up to do it again for the next 6 days. The one day I would have off I was too exhausted to meet my spiritual, physical or emotional needs or my children's. I was down-casted and weighed down, devoid of purpose, dignity, spirit, and soul, until I met my spiritual navigator, Kristine, and encountered her healing practice.

Cancer forced me to face my core beliefs about who I am, my place in the world, and my relationship with the universe. It was the ultimate trust exercise. This flood in my life that could've drowned me, gave me my rainbow in the form of Kristine. Through her knowledge, insight, wisdom and her healing practices, she has assisted in physically, mentally and spiritually recovering me from the various harrowing side effects of cancer! After 3 months of radiation, 6 months of chemotherapy, esophageal reconstructive surgery, and physical therapy, I found Kristine's practice be the most effective in actually relieving the pain. She taught visualization techniques to move past the pain towards healing, which has even healed my mind from doubt, and filled my spirit with an abundance of hope, light, love, and anticipation of life's goodness.

Kristine is one of those people that you meet and know that you have encountered a wise soul, a sage, an evolved being, blessed with intuitive gifts and healing hands. She is a guide who turned on my spiritual flashlight, dispelling darkness and shining a healing light. I'm a practicing Catholic, and she was able to relate to my faith. Her life and words are infused with healing power, which was so refreshing. I found her to be a caring, compassionate healer with a divine purpose of guiding people through their specific needs in life's transitions and journey's; leading us from tragedies to triumphs. She has blessed my mind and soul with the knowledge that either there will be something solid to stand on, or you will be taught how to fly! Kristine has been my flight instructor in the recognition of God's love and path for my life; helping me to stand in that balance of co-creation and surrender to the events, gifts, grace, and will of each and every day. In our sessions she lifted and enlightened my soul, and my life. A true gift! Her healing powers have the ability to reach whatever place you are at, to touch and transform you. Her abilities will speak to your heart through the pages in this book. You won't just read her words; you will feel it. This book will enhance your earths journey and beyond; to help you to soar towards the heavens and fill the spaces in your life that require healing, peace, purpose, love, and light. I am eternally grateful to have been blessed with her divine presence in my life.

—Denise Ingram
Single mother
Cancer survivor
BSW-Social Worker

INTRODUCTION

Whatever we plant in our subconscious mind and nourish with repetition and emotion will one day become reality.

—*Earl Nightingale*

The Ills of Modern Life

As the technology of our modern world continues to advance, it seems to leave our happiness in the dust. Today, people are plagued with unprecedented levels of stress, depression, anxiety, disease, addiction, divorce, and many other ills. More than ever, we and our friends and loved ones report feeling lost, hating our careers, and suffering from a void within that leads to embracing all manner of addictions. What's worse, these negative emotions can also manifest in the body as physical "dis-ease" or illnesses such as cancer.

What few people realize is that all these negative emotions and the physical health problems they create are caused by the illusion of fear, or False Evidence Appearing Real, in our lives.

Because fear is the opposite of love, it is the first sign of disconnection between the self and our own spirituality, or Source.

Fears not only limit us from experiencing heaven on Earth but also cause us to believe that we are alone and disconnected from our authentic selves. In adopting this illusory belief, we forget that we are one with the universe.

We lose sight of the fact that we are spirits having a human experience—and not the other way around.

You and your loved ones may be experiencing these ills yourselves. These emotions all stem from feeling disconnected from Source—our reason for being here in the first place. So many people live their lives in physical and emotional suffering, denying their own innate wisdom and spiritual truth. You, yourself, may be one of them.

But what if you didn't have to live this way?

The Healing Power of Source Energy

You can live free from negative emotions and the physical health challenges they cause. All you need to do to live a healthier and happier life is look to and reconnect with your spiritual center, which many people think of as God, for healing energy. I call this spiritual center Source or authentic self.

Reconnecting with Source means giving up living life through struggle. From the moment you took your first breath, your soul's purpose has been to embark on a journey of fulfillment and joy. This journey is one that each one of us is able to take, if we only commit ourselves to its path. At the end of that path is a doorway to magic and transformation, just waiting to open for you.

Now is your time to finally say yes to that still voice inside your heart that has continually been whispering and painting the perfect picture of your dream life—a life filled with the manifestation of joy, love, health, happiness, and prosperity. This is what is possible when you reconnect with your authentic self.

This is a transformation that I myself have undergone and have, in turn, guided hundreds of my clients through. Once you tap into that energy, your life becomes effortless. Things that you once believed were impossible to achieve or experience suddenly become possible. Relationships that you never thought could be healed grow stronger with renewed purpose and commitment. Illusions and dis-ease dissolve from the body.

There is no limit to what can be achieved through reconnection with Source. The universe is extremely literal, just like a genie. What you wish for is what you manifest.

Prepare yourself for a journey of spiritual reconnection that will heal your mind, body, and spirit.

A Guide along Your Path to Healing

I am able to help guide others along the path to healing because I too started out where they are now: seemingly stuck in an unfulfilling life. For many years, I found myself caught up in the illusion of a fear-based reality, allowing myself to live disconnected from Source and feeling empty inside of myself. It took me a long time to reconnect with my own spirituality and find my true path. But once I broke free from that illusion and found the courage to create my own path, trusting Source to guide me, my life transformed very quickly.

Like many people, I lived the first thirty years of my life trying to fit into what was expected of me by society. In order to do this, I had to forget what I knew as a child: being connected with Source. During the years that I allowed myself to experience this spiritual disconnection, I too was filled with fear, anger, resentment, addictions, and unforgiveness.

It wasn't until I hit rock bottom that all of that changed for me. Eventually, my troubles came to a head, and at a point in my life where I began to entertain thoughts of suicide, I remembered the connection I'd felt to Source when I was young. Finally, at this terrible low point, I surrendered to the universe, opening the floodgates and reconnecting to the spiritual truth, mission, and purpose I was meant to follow in this lifetime.

For me, that mission has been helping others to heal themselves, which in turn became the path to my own healing. Once I dedicated myself to the journey of the unknown, miracles filled my life. The very techniques discussed in this book are the ones I have worked with to find my own path to healing, and now I work with them to help seekers just like you, as they walk the path of their own healing journeys.

How to Use This Book to Heal Yourself

This book has been written as a roadmap for your path to healing. By the time you turn the last few pages, you will have gained the wisdom needed to find the secret to living a blissful life. The combination of divine wisdom, practical knowledge, and recommended techniques, therapies, and other tools set down in the following pages will help jumpstart your own healing journey.

Because what I discuss in each new chapter builds upon knowledge gained in previous chapters, I suggest that you read each one in the order it is presented the first time you read this book. Then, later down the road, you can revisit specific chapters as needed when roadblocks such as fear, anger, or depression crop up along your path.

The best thing about communicating with you through this book is that it enables me to help you experience healing and awaken your own gifts and abilities in the comfort of your own home.

Through our own awakening and healing, we increasingly shift the energy on Mother Earth to a greater awareness of love and peace.

In reading this book, you will gain the tools you need to over-come the illusions that have been holding you back. In turn, you will be guided towards a life filled with joy, happiness, health, and prosperity by bringing balance to your love life, health, career, and finances. The key to all of this is to achieve a balanced mind, body, and spirit.

By using the tools in this book, you will tap into the power you have within yourself to live a fulfilled life. This book will help you to not only heal your emotions, thoughts, and physical body, but also release old patterns tied to fearful belief systems and heal on mental, emotional, and spiritual levels.

You will learn to live a life *free* from anxiety, stress, depression, physical ailments, fears, anger, resentment, unforgiveness, and addiction. Through trust, faith, patience, and determination, I found myself and my purpose. I trust that this book will help you find yours.

A life of purpose, happiness, and wellness is within your reach. Embark on this journey of healing with me, and I will show you the path to the life you choose to live.

Chapter 1

Preparing for Your Journey of Healing

We are not human beings having a spiritual experience.
We are spiritual beings having a human experience.

—*Pierre Teilhard de Chardin*

The Path to True Healing

When our souls come into the physical world, over time, earthly illusions drag us away from the true essence of who we are. These illusions manifest through addictions to sex, alcohol, or drugs. They may also turn into physical dis-ease in the body such as cancer, heart conditions, weight issues, insomnia, high blood pressure, emotional problems, and more.

Faced with such ailments, we turn to prescription medications, desperately trying to reverse the effects of the illusion that has taken root in our bodies and minds. Ultimately, this only leads to more problems. While stuck in this vicious cycle, what we often fail to recognize is that our bodies and minds are intelligent organisms. As such, they heal best through the use of natural resources, such as plants and meditation.

We are a society addicted to quick fixes to patch any and all mental or physical ailments. When we have a skin issue, such as a rash, cut, or burn, we turn to ointments or creams to cover it up. Similarly, we turn to medications to stop diarrhea, vomiting, or constipation, or even to stop ourselves from feeling emotions that—as humans—we need to allow ourselves to feel, work through, and release.

By failing to recognize and trust the intelligence of our minds and bodies, we disconnect ourselves from Source and destroy any chance our minds and bodies have to truly heal.

Your body is your sanctuary. By allowing yourself to release what does not belong in your sanctuary, you can allow the innate intelligence of your system to do what it does best: heal itself.

This is also true in cases of dis-ease, even with serious illnesses such as cancer. During my life and work, I have witnessed many spontaneous miracles of healing from cancer and other physical ailments that occurred when the individual surrendered and allowed the intelligence of his or her own body to take charge and heal itself. This occurs when the mind, body, and spirit come into harmony with each other and Source.

In this chapter, you will learn how to recognize the signs of being disconnected from Source, and how to apply fundamental spiritual principles to your own life to facilitate your own healing. I'll also break down the topics for each chapter that follows, so that you can get a sense of where we're headed as you take your first steps along your path to healing.

Your journey toward spiritual wholeness and unending joy has begun. As our first step on the path, let's make sure we're on the same page when we talk about Source and spirit.

What Is Spirituality?

Life is a journey during which the soul continually seeks to express its divine self. During this time in human history, however, many people make the mistake of confusing spirituality with religious doctrine.

To clarify, spirituality is not a religion. It is that quiet space deep inside of us. It is the light within us where the gentle guiding wisdom of Source resides. It is our inner voice, or our intuition, which always speaks the truth.

Spirituality is the calm awareness that allows us to remain in the present moment, the part of ourselves that frees us from judgment, blame, guilt, and fear. It patiently waits for our signal of surrender to take us on a journey to our spiritual path—the unique path each of us is here to fulfill. Yet far too often, we fail to follow this guidance to love and be of service.

The beauty and peace of living a spiritually fulfilled life is accessible for each and every one of us, because at our core, we are all one with Source.

If you are currently seeking to find your truth and you believe there is more to life than what you are experiencing today, then you have already taken the first steps on your journey to enlightenment.

The next step is learning to connect more deeply with your own spirituality—your own natural link to Source.

The Three Commitments for Spiritual Connection

There are three commitments I invite you to observe in order to attain the life that you desire.

First, it is essential to change situations and relationships in your life that no longer work. The soul's purpose is to be and experience love in all areas of life. This means that if certain individuals in your life cause more harm than joy, then you must be ready to shift those relationships.

In order to heal from the illusions that are making you sick and unhappy, you must first disengage yourself from any unhealthy expectations or attachments—and most importantly, from the belief systems of other people that you may have adopted as your own. Disconnecting from toxic people and situations allows you to reconnect with your authentic self.

Once you have freed yourself of unhealthy attachments and expectations, the next step is to get clear about what it is that your spirit is calling you to do—your mission in this lifetime. To learn this, I invite you to write down—in whatever level of detail you desire—your goals and dreams.

What is it that you would love to experience in the areas of love, relationships, career, health, and finances?

Spend some time turning within to find the answers to this question and commit them to paper. Avoid focusing on the challenges you face and wish to be rid of and, instead, describe the kind of life you choose to live. Research shows that those who write down their dreams are ten times more likely to experience them. This is the Law of Attraction at work. We'll discuss this guiding law of the universe in more detail later on.

The final step of achieving spiritual reconnection is simply to have faith. You must start to believe that the universe is full of infinite possibilities and that it longs to bring you what you truly desire. What you desire and focus on is what you manifest and experience in life. Once you start believing that your dreams are truly possible and already on their way to you, they will begin to come true.

Often, the most challenging part of living by these three commitments is having the determination to change the situations and relationships that no longer work in our lives. This is difficult, because these same situations and relationships have often become part of who we think we are and where we believe we are headed.

In seeking to reconnect with Source and your own true path, you must first prepare yourself for the journey you are seeking to undertake. A big part of these preparations is accepting that it's time to make the necessary changes to live a life that offers more fulfillment and joy.

But before you can undertake your journey toward the life of your dreams, you must first identify the areas in your life in which you have become disconnected from.

How to Identify Spiritual Disconnection in Your Own Life

Many people live disconnected from their spiritual centers, but how can you tell if you are cutting yourself off from Source energy?

Most people believe that living a spiritual life of peace and love is out of reach for them. They are under the impression that in order to live this kind of life, they must be "gifted" or "chosen." For centuries, this has been the false message given to us by our religious leaders. This misconception has led many to become slaves to the fear of the ego mind, causing them to live meaningless and disconnected lives.

If you are not connecting to the beauty of nature and to the people around you, if you are not present in the moment to feel the gentle rush of the ocean waves and the breeze on your skin, if you are not present enough to see and feel the love that surrounds you, you are disconnected from yourself and Source.

If you persistently choose the path of the ego, the course of your life continues to feel like it is going against the current. Everything you do turns into an endless uphill battle for survival.

Life is a journey, and the soul naturally seeks to experience that journey authentically through every situation. When this need is not being met, you experience constant internal turmoil and dissatisfaction with the course of your life. This is the first and most powerful sign that you are disconnected from Source—and that your soul is trying to lead you to your desired life.

Because the soul continually strives to experience joy and fulfillment, these negative feelings will continue until you surrender your ego and give your spirit the joy and fulfillment it perpetually seeks. Surrendering and determining to change what no longer brings you fulfillment are important actions necessary to achieve a spiritually fulfilled life, or enlightenment.

The Breaking Point of Surrender

Surrender comes to all of us when we are most vulnerable—when we feel lost and, often alone. For so many of us, this moment comes only when we are at the lowest points in our lives, because of an addiction, the loss of a loved one, an illness, or mental distress.

For me, that moment came when I realized that the career I had initially chosen in life was bringing me nothing but sorrow. In 2008, after ten years of working as an accountant, I reached a crisis point in my life. I was surrounded by loving friends and family, but the beauty of those connections meant nothing to me, because I was consumed with the inner turmoil of hating the career that I was in. Over time, those negative emotions had begun to destroy me from the inside out.

Around this time, I began to experience severe, troubling emotional and physical symptoms that my doctor had no diagnosis for. He told me that at age twenty-eight, I had the medical chart of an eighty-year-old woman. All the symptoms I was having—headaches, intestinal issues, stomach problems, my arms and legs going numb, and being in chronic pain—seemed to have no apparent root cause.

By January 2009, I was deeply depressed and feeling hopeless. Then, one day at work, I got up out of my chair, turned to my coworkers, and said, "If I have to do this for the next thirty-plus years, I would rather die." Not surprisingly, they were stunned. They both paled, looking as if they'd seen a ghost.

At that moment, I experienced what I now know to be an out-of-body experience. It felt like my heart and soul were ripped out of my chest. In pure energy form, I found myself staring back at my physical body. And I knew that if I did not change something fast, I would pay a terrible price.

I later learned that all my symptoms were nothing but a result of body syndromes created by my own toxic thoughts. Finally, after a decade of suffering in a career that I didn't belong in, I surrendered to Source and asked for guidance. Only then was I able to reconnect with my authentic self to find the emotional, physical, and spiritual healing that I needed. That is when I finally set myself on my true path.

This was my point of total and complete surrender to Source by accepting and opening to the unknown.

Of course, the unknown is a scary thing to face. Too often, we would much rather stay in the dark and be miserable, because at least this state, even as awful as it can be, is in the realm of the known. Sometimes, stepping into the unknown by trying something new can seem even scarier than staying stuck in misery. But I am here to let you in on a secret: letting go of the need for control is required in order to gain more joy out of life.

Let go and allow yourself to be guided by the universe. Once you do, you will begin to see the light of countless opportunities shining in front of you. You may even realize that these opportunities were there all along, only before, you were simply unable to see them. When we are blinded by our illusions, we're too busy focusing on the darkness or chaos that surrounds us (often, rooted in negative past experiences) to see the infinite flow of opportunities available to us through our connection to Source.

By focusing on the present moment and the next step in the path ahead, you too can achieve an enlightened spiritual balance.

The Healing Power of Spiritual Enlightenment

The concept of enlightenment has been around for centuries, because this is the process through which we all grow spiritually. Even so, enlightenment is a concept that most people feel is far out of reach for them. I'm here to tell you that nothing could be further from the truth. Contrary to what many believe, you don't have to quit your job and move to a monastery to become enlightened.

But what does it really mean to live in harmony with your spiritual self?

Enlightenment simply means being focused more on being in the present moment, rather than giving our power and energy to the past or the future. Achieving this state can make a tremendous difference in your life. As research shows, those individuals who become enlightened are physically different from the rest of us. The entire molecular structure of their bodies shifts and changes.

This powerful shift has the ability to slow down the aging process and boost the immune system. It helps increase your body's frequency to a level where you are no longer prone to getting sick or becoming ill, because illness and negative thoughts vibrate on a lower energy level than the one you function at. This is possible once you have surrendered to living in the present moment and focusing your thoughts toward positive outcomes.

Achieving this energy balance within ourselves is especially crucial in our day and age, where cancer seems to spread quickly and no age group is safe from it. The reason for this sad reality is in large part because our society teaches us to live life in a state of constant fear. But as we've learned, that fear is simply another earthly illusion—the lie that we could ever be disconnected from Source.

In order to overcome this illusion, you need only commit to the journey to reconnect with who you are and what you are meant to be doing in this life. That journey begins with a commitment to achieving enlightenment, or a mindful focus on the present, rather than the past or the future.

Your Path Back to Source, Your Authentic Self

Now you have a growing sense of the shift in mindset you need in order to find the healing you seek, but the journey itself still lies ahead of you. As you undertake this journey to healing through reconnecting with Source energy, you may hit obstacles along the way. At each of these stops, you will be confronted with old, negative patterns of beliefs, emotions, and thoughts and challenged to flip these into positive new directions.

The good news is that you won't have to face these negative hurdles alone. In the chapters to come, I'll give you the tools, techniques, and outlook you need to overcome every possible challenge you may face, including the following:

Healing Disconnection. Overcome the negative emotions that result from living disconnected from your truth and mission, and regain a sense of connection to Source and purpose on your guided path.

Healing Fear. Learn how to stop allowing yourself to be steered by fear and instead be guided by the divine love of Source to regain control over the direction of your life.

Healing Stress, Anxiety, and Panic Attacks. Master techniques you can use to stop stress, anxiety, and panic attacks in their tracks, replacing these negative states with a calm and positive outlook through spiritual connection.

Healing Anger and Resentment. Release anger and resentment, and instead be guided forward along your journey by taking responsibility for your own thoughts, actions, and feelings.

Healing Depression. Learn techniques to combat and overcome depression, regaining the positive forward momentum of living a more joyful and fulfilled existence.

Healing Past-Life Attachments. Explore the techniques that will allow you to identify energies you've carried over into this life from your past existences, and learn the secret to integrating these as a powerful force of healing.

Healing Addiction. Identify the true cause of addictions, and find balance and harmony along your journey by reconnecting to Source.

Healing Unforgiveness. Release the toxic energy of unforgiveness, learning to heal old wounds by embracing a spirit of grace and forgiveness of those who have caused us harm.

Solutions for the Body, Mind, and Spirit. Boost your healing potential with these advanced solutions for truly empowered wellness that focus on the mind-body-spirit connection.

Finally, I will end by showing you how to take your healing journey to the next level, healing not only yourself, but also those around you.

Along the way, I'll also share with you stories from the healing journeys of my clients, so that you can learn and benefit from their experiences and the healing they have received. Please note that their names and some other details have been changed here in order to protect their privacy.

Picking up this book is one of the first steps of your own journey to healing. Once you've finished reading it, you will have gained the knowledge and tools you need to reconnect with Source, whose boundless healing energy will guide you to a better life filled with joy, happiness, health, and prosperity.

You too can live free from negative emotions and the physical health challenges they cause. The way forward is to reconnect with Source and awaken to your own healing gifts. Armed with trust, faith, patience, and determination, as well as the skills you will gain from reading this book, you will arrive at your journey's ultimate destination: the life you have always wanted to live.

Let's look at how to tackle the first obstacle that most of us face in getting there: the feeling of being lost to one's true self that results from living disconnected from Source.

Chapter 2

Healing Disconnection

When God sees you doing your part, developing what He has given you, then He will do His part and open doors that no man can shut.

—Unknown

The Consequences of Living Disconnected from Your True Self

The first time Samantha walked through the doors of the therapy room at the cancer center, she looked terrified. Tears rolled down her cheeks as she told me her story.

Sam was born into a family with high expectations for her. From when she was young, her parents dreamed that one day she would become an attorney. Sam grew up believing that, in order to keep her parents happy and make them proud, she had to fulfill their goals for her. So that's exactly what she set out to do.

And yet she dreaded her choice. Studying law and working toward passing the bar exam made her feel like she was going against the natural flow of her own energy. But it was what she felt she had to do, so she worked hard to make her parents' dream happen.

All through college and law school, Sam was miserable. And once she finally landed a corporate law job, instead of getting better, things got worse. She was finally able to start paying off her student loans, but she began to accrue even more debt. Like many people trapped in jobs they hate, Sam tried to fill the hole in her heart with more and more material goods. Instead of making her feel better, this only made her feel increasingly empty inside.

An outsider looking into her life shortly before this point would easily have believed Sam was living the perfect American dream. She had a good job, a loving husband, a newborn child, and parents who loved her. But inside, she was miserable.

Sam felt lost, surrounded on all sides by fear, worry, and doubt. Before long, she was spiraling down into a dark, never-ending hole. Having committed to living a life others had set for her—one she hated in many ways—she felt there was no place for the possibility of a dream of her own. And within two years of entering her law career, Sam suddenly fell ill. Soon she learned she had manifested cancer.

By embracing a path that was not true to her own spiritual nature, Sam disconnected herself from Source energy. The negative emotions resulting from this disconnection manifested in her life as emotional and physical ailments such as insomnia, intense fear of loss, and finally cancer.

After Sam vented her deepest fears and worries to me at the clinic, the key to her healing process became very clear to me. The thing that was making her sick was the illusion she had embraced about her own life purpose—her disconnection from Source. The solution was to help her release her fears, and to heal her insomnia through hypnotherapy. We also applied energy healing techniques to help her body rejuvenate and heal itself and mantras to retrain her mindset.

Because the mind can focus on only one energy and one thought at a time, I asked Sam to create and hold more positive thoughts for herself—thoughts about finding her true path and mission in this lifetime, about the life she chose to live. I told her to repeat the following mantra every time her fear popped up into her conscious mind: "With Source energy, I am powerful. My body and mind are vibrant, healthy, and strong." I also asked her to create a simple mantra of her own to focus on the positive energy needed to heal her mental and emotional state.

Mantras and energy healing turned out to be the perfect tools to help Sam free herself from the illusion that was making her sick. (If you're interested in seeing what guided mantras can do for your own healing, you can visit my website at www.journeystoheal.com for more information.)

Using these tools combined with traditional treatment, she turned her life around. She is now completely free from cancer and is happily enjoying every day of her life with her family.

The Power of Emotions

I've shared Sam's story with you because it illustrates the dangers of remaining disconnected from Source. In deciding to pursue law against the grain of her own interests and passions, not only was Sam not fulfilling her true spiritual purpose on this earth, but she also opened herself up to a host of emotional and physical illnesses. The reason for this is that Sam experienced powerful negative emotions as she struggled to conform to the role others had chosen for her. But rather than allow herself to feel and process these feelings, she buried them.

Our feelings are immensely powerful because they are of the soul, thus are the source to the positive force in our lives. Emotions, on the other hand, are of the ego, which control our thinking, behavior, actions, and most importantly, our experiences. Because of this, individuals who make the choice to ignore or suppress their emotions set themselves up for physical and emotional illness.

The main cause of spiritual disconnection is rooted in our attachment to negative emotions from our past experiences. We are spiritual and energetic beings living in an energetic universe. Because emotions affect us both mentally and physically, all of our experiences are influenced by the energy created by it. When we fail to work through and release our negative emotions, the resultant energy blockages affect the body's frequency, such as chakras and aura. This leads to diseases such as cancer, heart conditions, high blood pressure, and many other chronic illnesses.

Only by fully dealing with and letting go of negative emotions can we reconnect with Source and heal our hearts, minds, and spirits. In this chapter, I'll share some of my own experiences of disconnection with you, as well as that of another client of mine. I'll also cover some techniques and tools that you can use to determine whether you are experiencing disconnection in your own life, and how to appropriately and fully process your emotions in order to reconnect with your authentic self.

Once you have reestablished your soul's natural connection to Source energy, you'll be prepared for the next step toward finding your true purpose to live a happier, healthier, and more fulfilled life.

Your journey toward healing has begun.

My Own Struggle with Disconnection

The first time I looked into Sam's eyes, I saw a vision of my past self: tired, sick, and desperate for a sense of purpose and meaning in my own life.

Before I started on my spiritual path, I too was lost and disconnected from myself and Source. I come from a culturally fear-based Christian family, and my parents had great expectations of me. Their vision of a successful life for me included a college degree followed by a successful career, marriage, and children. They made it clear to me at a young age that they expected me to become an engineer, attorney, doctor, or accountant when I grew up. Though none of these careers resonated with me, I resigned myself to complying with my family's wishes.

For years, I struggled and kept swimming against the current, changing from one major to the next until, finally, I settled on a business degree with a career in accounting. By the time I graduated from college, I had already changed accounting jobs twice and was starting to feel hopeless. It was then that I began to lose my sense of who I was. The only thing I was sure of was that I enjoyed helping others feel better by, teaching or mentoring them.

I tried to convince myself that I was happy. But I was keenly aware of the emptiness I felt deep in my heart. When I heard others say, "When you love what you do, it turns into gold," my heart and soul would jump out of my chest, longing to know what that felt like. As I journeyed along, I mentally accepted the struggle and emptiness I had come to know as a permanent part of my life. Still, my heart and soul were far from giving in to this illusion.

Nonetheless, this routine of barely surviving went on for the next five years. And all the while, I continued to get more and more frustrated with myself. Why did I feel so empty inside? Why could I not find fulfillment in my accounting career? I continued to move from one accounting firm to another.

By age thirty, I was married and about to have my second child. On the outside, my life looked like a fairytale dream come true. But on the inside, my mental and physical health was deteriorating. Day in and day out, I struggled with the void in my soul and hiding my feelings from the people I trusted and loved the most. As a result, I became increasingly detached from my husband and children.

Soon, my growing desperation manifested physically in my body, leading me down a path of self-destruction. I started losing my eyesight. My right arm developed nerve damage. Due to my high levels of stress and anxiety, my internal organs were unable to function in a balanced way. I experienced constant migraine headaches, and my mental and emotional state was going haywire.

But even then, unbeknownst to me, my heart and soul were preparing me for my true purpose.

My Road Back to Healing

For most of my life, I had felt like a fish out of water, trying to survive in a waterless and false reality that was foreign to me. So

I kept flapping around, trying to find where I belonged—all the while not realizing that the place I was looking for was the eternal pool of divine truth. But I was destined to follow that plan, and once I awoke to this truth, I became determined to fulfill my highest purpose.

Once I connected to that microscopic pinpoint of light and hope in my soul, I knew I would never go back. I made a commitment to stop being a victim and to take responsibility for my own life and experiences. The moment that I surrendered, my heart opened to release the pain from the past and welcome the divine truth, to live each day of my life as if it were the last.

Prior to my surrender, my world was unfulfilling and dark. Afterward, my life transformed and blossomed like a lotus flower in a beautiful pond. In less than five years, my life path and relationships flourished into something magical. When I awakened and reconnected to my spiritual path, it transformed my relationships and my life, filling both with joy, happiness, health, and endless possibilities.

The moment I gave my heartfelt commitment to live life mindfully, positive changes and divine guidance began to pour in. I became so encouraged by my own success that I wanted to share it with the world, guiding my clients to reconnect with their inner truth. I was prepared to take on the journey to push beyond my boundaries and limiting beliefs.

It was only then that, for the first time in my life, I began to truly see the beauty, wonderment, and magic of life that surrounded me. Within the first three years of embarking upon my spiritual path, I experienced more success and fulfillment in helping heal others than I had in more than a decade in my accounting career. I had finally awakened to the life I was meant to lead and was able to see this as a gift from the universe.

Reconnection with Source through Living Mindfully

To reconnect with Source, you need only learn to live mindfully and in the present moment. In the last chapter, you learned that this is the definition of becoming enlightened. Achieving enlightenment is not an easy task, but it is possible for everyone. And as I mentioned before, you don't need to be "special" or "the chosen one" to get there.

Living mindfully simply means experiencing conscious awareness of the present moment with an open mind. Being aware of the present moment connects us with ourselves and allows us to appreciate the beauty of all that is around us. This simple yet powerful process helps us to become aware of suppressed experiences or memories and to safely navigate through and release them.

Mindfulness provides unlimited benefits, but the most important thing it offers is the ability to release limiting beliefs to live a fulfilled life.

The more you bring yourself back to the present moment and focus on positives and gratitude, the more powerful your awareness becomes. When this state of awareness is permanently achieved, it becomes a state of being. You'll begin to see everything around you—from nature to your own personal experiences—as being perfect just the way it is. Every experience teaches you something new about yourself and helps you grow spiritually, which is the ultimate truth of life.

In addition to living mindfully, it is also vital to remember to allow yourself to ask Source for the healing you need.

Permission to Ask

Another client of mine, Julie, had just returned for her third session with me at the cancer center. She had been diagnosed with cancer several months prior to our first meeting. During our first two sessions, Julie had shed many tears of sadness and frustration. But on this day, her eyes were filled with tears of joy and excitement.

The minute she got comfortable, she began by saying how blessed she felt to have finally given herself the chance to shift her beliefs from being fear based. At last, she was learning to embrace her spirituality and heal. As she spoke and cried freely, I held her hands to comfort her.

Then she told me something about her past that made her current situation clearer. Julie had come from humble beginnings. She was one of eight children, and her parents often told her she should not bother asking for what she wanted, because she wouldn't get it. This led to a painful and limiting belief for Julie: a mindset of feeling that she shouldn't and couldn't ask for what she needed for herself.

She thanked me for giving her permission to let go and let the universe guide her, and she said she had finally asked Source for healing. I reminded her that it was not I who had given her permission to open up; she had given *herself* permission to ask for and receive healing. It was her willingness to ask for help that allowed the universe to guide her toward that healing light.

As our cognitive therapy session came to an end, I prepared Julie for her energy healing session. I asked her not to force, but to allow the divine energy of love to flow through her and bring her the miracle of healing. Next, I asked her to take a deep breath and close her eyes while I placed my hands on top of her head and centered myself.

The minute my hands touched her head, something amazing started to happen. The energy around us shifted. It felt as if we were enveloped in a bubble of bliss, love, and light. I allowed my physical body to act as a conduit to transfer this bliss, love, and healing to her physical body. A minute later, her chest started to rise up in a way that seemed impossible, even if she was taking a deep, cleansing breath.

As I opened my eyes to see what was happening to her body, I noticed her breathing was normal, and yet her chest kept rising up about four inches toward the ceiling. Then it would slowly move down. This process continued for about five minutes.

At this point, I wanted to make sure Julie was comfortable experiencing this. When I looked at her face, I noticed a blissful smile and tears rolling down her cheeks like pearls. I sensed that she was in a place of love, bliss, and peace, and that I was not to interrupt that process. So I closed my eyes again and continued to serve as the channel to bring this healing energy of love into her body.

This entire process continued for the next fifteen minutes. Finally, the universe nudged me that it was time to come back into the present moment and reassured me that Julie's healing would continue even when she left that sacred space. At this point, I prepared her to come back into the present and share her experience with me.

The minute she opened her eyes, more tears started to flow, and she said that although the rising of her chest was a new experience for her, it felt genuine and safe. She also mentioned that during that process she felt life being poured into her lungs and body. This was something she had never felt before. We expressed our gratitude to Source for this healing, and weeks later, she came back with miraculous news: after her most recent medical tests, the doctors ruled that she no longer had active cancer cells in her body.

In giving herself permission to ask for healing from the universe, Julie reconnected with Source energy, thereby freeing herself from the limiting beliefs that were making her sick.

The Healing Power of Connection with Source

The power to heal and be healed is locked inside of each one of us. But only through reconnecting with our authentic selves or Source can this potential be freed.

The combination of guided meditation and hypnosis, along with energy healing, mantras, and EFT, allowed this particular client to become free from her fears and burdens, and to receive healing. Most importantly, she learned to ask for healing from Source.

As the Law of Attraction and teachings of many spiritual masters state, "Ask and believe that you have already received." Never allow the ego's fears of the unknown dictate your life experiences, because if you allow this, those fears will overpower you. Instead, connect with your higher self, take your power back, and co-create the beautiful journey of your life with Source.

The most important aspect of managing your emotions is first to pinpoint what part of your life is causing your negative emotions. Then you must take baby steps to correct that which does not serve your highest good.

In learning how to reconnect with Source, you've now taken the first big step along your own beautiful journey to healing. If you practice mindfulness and awareness of the present, and release toxic relationships, negative situations, and limiting old belief systems, you too can tap into the miraculous healing power, your own spiritual connection to Source.

In addition to allowing herself to feel and process her negative emotions to reestablish her connection with Source, part of Julie's healing journey required releasing old fears that were holding her back. We'll talk more about the power of long-held fears and how to overcome them in the next chapter.

Chapter 3

Healing Fear

The only place that fear can exist is in our thoughts of the future. It is a product of our imagination causing us to fear things that are not present, and may never exist. That is near insanity. Don't misunderstand me, danger is real, but fear is a choice.

—*Will Smith*

Allowing Trust to Overcome Fear

As I began to talk with a new client, Denise the amazing woman who wrote the foreword for this book, I intuitively knew that what she was telling me and what was really going on inside of her were very different. In order to help her find healing, I would first have to help her be able to trust—not just me, but herself and Source. With this in mind, I gradually eased her into telling me what really was bothering her.

Denise had been diagnosed with throat cancer and was in her final stages of treatment. For the past two months, she'd had an excruciating pain on the left side of her head. The pain included her left ear, which had been ringing nonstop since the pain began. She was also having trouble with her sense of balance. While telling me her symptoms, Denise began to cry and open up to me further. She was suffering from intense fear that her cancer might have come back. She was terribly afraid that the pain in her ear meant that the cancer had now manifested in her brain.

Because she had already demonstrated herself to be a very spiritual person (speaking of God's plan for her and acknowledging this as the way to go), I first helped her calm down by telling her that she was safe and secure, because she was protected by God. Then I asked her to focus on her faith in God, rather than giving power to her fear. Only then could she find the healing she needed.

Once Denise was calm, I received divine guidance telling me to offer her an energy healing session. Although she seemed skeptical, Denise was so desperate to get rid of her pain that she agreed to try this. She was having difficulty balancing herself, so I helped her get up onto the massage table. Then I started the session the same way I begin every time: I said a quick prayer asking the divine light to surround us and to use me as the vessel to bring her healing.

At first, nothing seemed different. My hands hovered over her body, scanning its energy field and following where the energy took me. But five minutes into the session, Denise told me that the inside of her body felt very warm. Then, suddenly, she felt a tremendous feeling of love pour into her heart and start moving up toward her head.

When the heat reached the left side of her head and her ear, she called out to me, "Oh my God, Kristine. It hurts. I can't take this pain. It's too much." I was in a trance state, just trusting that Source and the collective energies of the universe were at work.

But then I heard a voice say to me, "Tell her it gets worse before it gets better." I passed the message on to her, and she took a deep breath and relaxed.

Eventually, Denise felt a coolness replace the warmth, and her body jerked. She felt a loud pop in her left ear, and the pain ended. I felt the collective energy pull back and tell me I could finish up now. So I brought my hands into a prayer pose once again and thanked Source and all the energies from the light for their presence, love, and healing.

When we both opened our eyes, Denise sat up and got off the massage table herself. Then she turned to me and gave me the biggest hug. She pulled back and said, "I can't believe it. That horrible pain and the ringing in my ear are completely gone."

In this miraculous case, all it took was our faith and trust to allow the miracle of healing to show up for Denise in a single forty-minute energy healing session. Several years have passed since then, and now Denise is happy, healthy, and enjoying her new career and her beautiful family.

Understanding Fear

As Denise learned that day, fear—and the health problems it brings on—can be banished by trust and faith in the healing power of Source. This is because fear is the opposite of love. When we connect to Source energy and commit to fulfilling our true purpose on this earth, we are centered in universal love—and fear has no place in our lives.

But before we can do this, we must first release our fears.

And pinning fear down in order to release it can be tricky. The reason for this is that fear wears many disguises. Emotions such as anger, resentment, depression, stress, anxiety, and unforgiveness are each, at their core, mere symptoms of deeper, underlying fear.

In the introduction, I explained the true nature of fear: False Evidence Appearing Real. The illusion of fear is created by the ego, and its purpose is to disconnect you from your authentic self. This disconnection caused by living in fear forces you to forget who you are: a spirit having a physical, human experience.

As long as we feed our fear with the power of our thoughts, it will continue to exist and take us on a downward spiral. Left unchecked, fear can truly cripple us. Its negative effects cause stress on the mind and body, which ultimately allow physical illusions of dis-ease to manifest. This is because the body simply complies with what the mind is creating through its thoughts. Long-term fear and stress eventually bring on bowel problems, insomnia, headaches, allergies, stroke, and many other dis-eases.

By creating thoughts of fear, we give our spiritual power to that illusion, therefore telling our mind and soul that we are powerless against the fear, which is far from the truth.

And yet, a simple daily choice has the power to help you overcome fear.

By surrendering yourself to divine guidance, you can receive the healing needed to purge the emotional and physical effects of living in fear. In this chapter, I'll show you how to release old fears through the power of faith and trust in Source. I'll also share more of my own journey of healing.

My Early Experience of Fear

Unfortunately, most of us are born into and raised in fear-based belief systems that trap us in the illusion of fear. Day in and day out, it becomes increasingly difficult to free the self from this illusion. It becomes part of our behaviors, thoughts, and that false sense of self seems very real.

Growing up, I allowed my family and surroundings to instill a tremendous amount of fear in me. Like a poison, this fear trickled down to almost every aspect of my life. The worst of these fears revolved around worshipping God and never doing wrong—so that God wouldn't "punish" me.

For most of my youth, I struggled with the idea of a God of retribution and punishment. I preferred to believe in a God that leads us toward love, peace, and joy. Even as a child, I believed that God is love—a universally divine Source energy that does not punish, judge, or condemn.

Over time, I realized that our fear-based experiences are rooted in the negative thoughts and toxicity around us. We are energy beings. Every thought created in the mind is energy. Therefore, when you experience positive thoughts, you will experience that which you are focusing on and putting your energy into.

Similarly, if you are prone to creating negative thoughts, that toxic energy attracts more of the same, building up into stress that leads to dis-ease or other life challenges, such as addictions. When I realized this truth, I was determined to change my negative thought patterns in order to experience a more meaningful life.

I started my spiritual journey by putting my trust and faith in the only thing that I knew could help me understand the mystery of life: my divine self. At the outset of this journey, it became clear to me that if I was unable to let go of my fears, I would not be able to pursue this new life that the universe had placed in my path.

But my fears had ruled my life for so long that, at first, I didn't know how to release them.

I began to find the answer to this question in deep meditation and healing ceremonies. During the first six months of my journey, I dedicated myself to these practices, and through them, I was able to find that channel of connection where no fear can ever be present or survive. Part of this process also meant freeing myself of any expectation about what was about to happen. I simply allowed myself to go within, because I knew nothing would change until I surrendered to the truth of who I am and what I represent as pure spirit.

This meant digging though my past and bringing to the surface all the emotions and thoughts I had long kept suppressed. I had to peel away those layers one by one, like an onion. Through this process, over time, I began to pierce the fear-based illusions I had come to believe as part of my reality. It was only then that I came up against fear's greatest weapon against us: the negative thoughts of the ego mind.

Don't get me wrong; some levels of fear, such as not to run in front of moving cars or jump off a bridge without a parachute, are healthy, but when your ego uses fear to paralyze your daily life, it becomes unhealthy on many levels.

The Higher Self versus the Ego

The most challenging part of overcoming fear is gaining control of negative chatter in the mind or, in other words, taming the ego.

But before we can understand what it means to tame the ego, first we must fully understand the difference between the ego and the higher self. Your higher self is the part of you that is forever connected to Source, and because of this, it operates from a place of all-knowing wisdom. Your higher self always guides you to your highest potential.

Your ego, on the other hand, operates from very limited information—much of it based on earthly illusions that masquerade as reality. This is because the ego is the part of you that has chosen to be separate and independent from Source energy. Your ego spends much of its time creating unnecessary chatter in the mind. It's not that the act of thinking itself is bad. But when your thoughts are focused negatively on fear and self-doubt, this does not serve your highest purpose. And, unfortunately, thoughts rooted in fear and self-doubt are the ego's specialty.

For this reason, learning to tame the ego simply means being a conscious observer of our own thoughts. When ego-driven thoughts of fear and self-doubt pop up, the solution is to acknowledge that negative energy, allow it to pass, and then create a positive thought, using this to overwrite the negative one.

When I first started using this technique, I wasn't sure if it would really work; it seemed far too simple to be effective. Of course, this negative chatter itself was the work of my ego mind. Despite my skepticism, I decided to try the technique anyway.

My thought was, what have I got to lose? As I practiced this, each time a negative thought pattern popped in, I replaced it with a positive thought.

The effects were amazing.

The positive thoughts I held in my mind quickly proved to be a powerful force. I started seeing results almost immediately, as more and more positive energy was drawn into my day-to-day life experience, launching me on my new journey. With every meditation, I gained a sense of self-control that I had been lacking before.

As I dove deeper into this new energy, all sorts of fantastic new situations and opportunities showed up in my life. By embracing these new experiences, I was able to expand my knowledge and skills and prepare myself for my mission to help others heal. But this was possible for me only after I learned to shut down that ego mind chatter rooted in fear and self-doubt. Once I was able to free myself of fear-based thought patterns, I connected more deeply to Source and was able to begin to receive healing.

Whenever you go through a tough time, whether it's connected to love, career, finances, or relationships, you may feel that the negative experience broke your heart and soul, but this is far from the truth. One of the biggest spiritual messages I have received from the universe is the remembrance that our hearts and souls never suffer, break, or hurt. Our hearts and souls are from the universal light, and they do not know pain, suffering, hurt, or lack. It is simply our egos that are being crushed when we lose our love, careers, or financial security. To remedy this emotion is to not allow our egos to control or limit our lives and experiences. Careers, love relationships, and finances come and go, but the truth remains that as long as we keep our hearts open and continue to pour love and passion into our daily life experiences, we will always conquer all obstacles, and more love will show up in our lives.

The Healing Power of Releasing Fear

Through daily practice of prayer, meditation, and positive thinking, you too can cast off the illusions of fear. With the power of faith, miraculous healing through reconnection with your infinite self is within reach.

Let your life and experiences be the river that takes you along on a beautiful journey of healing. Don't let fear lead you to go against the current of this river, directing your life experiences. Instead, begin to trust Source and yourself. Follow in the direction of the current. With love in your heart, you have the power to achieve healing on every level, as nothing is impossible in the eyes of the divine. The word impossible means I'm Possible.

We have become so absorbed by the superficial world that we often fail to feel or hear our inner truth. What's more, we continually seek truth outside of ourselves, when in reality, Source dwells within every single one of us. Through prayer and meditation, you can reconnect with the divine and directly receive its blessings and miracles.

Even when we feel a sense of disconnection, as we discussed in the last chapter, we are never truly disconnected from Source. But as we go about our everyday lives, we often move away from the truth of who we are, growing more distant from this divine guidance. That truth of who we are is spirit, and through the power of our positive thoughts we are capable of manifesting unlimited greatness and success in all areas of our lives.

In order to change the outcome of our experiences, we must change the cause. If we are filled with fear, anger, hate, unforgiveness, envy, and judgment, we attract all forms of negativity and dis-ease to ourselves. We must work on the subconscious level of our minds, changing and shifting our thoughts from negative to positive.

This not only reconnects us to our higher selves, but it also changes how we act in negative situations in the future. Through this subconscious work, you will learn that by changing the energy of your thoughts, you change your life.

Over the past decade, my trust in Source energy has provided ample rewards, as I have patiently guided hundreds of my clients to release their fears of specific situations and people. Surrendering your fears invites divine intervention and the miracle of healing. The stories of miraculous healing I've shared so far in these pages, as well as those still to come, are a living example of the power of the universal Law of Attraction that guides you to your heart's desire.

To put this law into action in your life, write down your goals and dreams in the present tense, as if you already have them and live them. Read this list every night and every morning, when your subconscious is most suggestible. This will help you to stay mindful in thinking and speaking about what you choose to experience, and to openly surrender yourself to Source, allowing your dreams to manifest.

This practice will also help you to release your fears, as well as other illusions, assisting you in moving forward on your path to healing and reconnecting you with your true purpose. Remember, Source or God is extremely literal, and the energy of thoughts you send into the universe responds back with the exact same energy. It has a boomerang effect; what you put in is what you receive in return. In the next chapter, I discuss the roles that stress and anxiety play in blocking our forward progress, teaching you how to move past these obstacles along the course of your journey.

Once you learn to release these fear-based illusions, you can live a life of unlimited joy, happiness, health, and peace.

Chapter 4

Healing Stress, Anxiety, and Panic Attacks

The greatest weapon against stress is our ability to choose one thought over another.

—William James

Surrendering Stress and Anxiety to Source

When I received the first call from Joe, his fearful illusions had already grown so enormous that he felt he was being suffocated. He couldn't see a way out of this state, and the resulting stress was driving him to experience panic attacks.

When he walked in for his first session, I saw a tall, handsome middle-aged man, but his tense body language revealed his inner turmoil. Joe began our conversation by telling me he had always lived his life driven by logic. In fact, he was surprised he had even considered trying alternative therapies to find healing, but at this point, he was desperate.

The details of his external life seemed like something an average person in our society would dream of living. Joe was a very successful businessman with a strong family life and an abundance of material luxury. But internally, he felt dead, disconnected, fearful, anxious, and stressed out all the time. Nothing and no one was able to fulfill him or bring him joy. He felt as if he were stuck in an elevator that was moving only in one direction: down.

In short, Joe was ready to give it all up, but at the same time, he was in terrible fear of losing everything.

In our first session, I mostly concentrated on explaining to Joe that we are spiritual beings having a human experience, and that his situation was merely his soul crying out to shift his logical ways and reconnect with his higher self. Only then would he begin to see the truth of what was real in his life, which was all the love that surrounded him.

During the cognitive part of our session, I gently guided him to recognize that he was already in total surrender mode, and that this is the first step in allowing divinity to inspire us to shift and change our ways. I also explained that surrender is not giving up or giving our power away. Through surrender, we join forces with Source and the flow of the universe. That is when we can begin to go with the current instead of against it.

"Surrender" seemed like the magic word Joe was waiting to hear. This was his ticket to letting go of control.

For the next few months, Joe and I worked together through spiritual meditations, hypnotherapy, and exercises I assigned for his specific needs. We also used Emotional Freedom Technique (EFT) to release old beliefs and adopt new and healthier ones. This allowed him to feel safer, more secure, and more accepting of himself. By using these techniques, Joe was able to reconnect with himself and his family.

In addition to surrender, self-love also played a huge role in his healing. Before Joe could heal from the stress and anxiety plaguing his happiness and peace of mind, he had to learn to love and respect himself. In allowing himself to come first, he also learned to better love his family and truly be present with them. Now he is living life more mindfully, enjoying the success he has created for himself and his loved ones. He no longer experiences the fear, stress, anxiety, or panic attacks he once suffered from, because he now understands the importance of self-love.

In surrendering to the divine, Joe learned to live life to the fullest by living in the present moment. He also embraced one of the most important lessons in learning to release fear, stress, and anxiety: that no one has to worry about the future, because no one knows what the future will bring.

Understand Stress, Anxiety, and Panic Attacks

Like Joe, many of us in our modern, materialistic society face the damaging effects of stress on a daily basis. First thing in the morning, most people are programmed to wake up to the excruciating noise of an alarm clock. And yet this is one of the most disturbing ways you can start your day. When the body and mind are in a peaceful state, as in sleep, they need to awaken to a full state of consciousness in a gentle way, rather than being startled out of this state by a loud noise.

Stress is a silent killer. Starting your day in a state of stress not only elevates your blood pressure but also increases your heart rate, causing many people to think they are having anxiety attacks. This type of stress also tenses up all the muscles in the body and slows down both digestion and the metabolism. When this happens, cortisol is released into the body. The constant release of this hormone is damaging in the long run. It causes the body to accumulate fat around the abdomen, and it also drains your precious energy.

Chronic failure to overcome this kind of stress creates chaos in the immune system, lowering the body's energetic frequency level. And unfortunately, when the immune system is compromised, this leads to dis-eases in the body such as cancer, heart problems, sleepless nights, addictions, aches and pains, and many other illusions.

Because stress has such a negative impact on the body's systems, it's vital to find ways to reduce your stress level. To start, I encourage you to find a more gentle and creative way to begin your day. Instead of waking up to the sound of an annoying alarm clock, change this to something more soothing. Chances are that your smart phone, if you have one, offers apps that will wake you with gentle flashing lights or sounds. This simple technique is easy to implement and will dramatically decrease your stress level and tendency toward road rage early in the morning.

If you feel waking up to a traditional alarm clock is the only option that works for you, then at least start your day with a quick five- to ten-minute meditation to create peace in the mind and body. This will increase the effectiveness of your immune system as well as raise your body's energy frequency levels. Simply close your eyes and focus on the center of your forehead, where your third eye is. Visualize or think of something that creates an instant feeling of joy and love in your heart, mind, and body. Consciously choose the path to a stress-free life.

Changing the way you begin your day can have a powerful effect on your overall level of stress.

In this chapter, I'll share other techniques for stress relief and combatting panic and anxiety, as well as stories from the lives of my clients and my own experiences that illustrate the healing power of reconnecting with Source. Armed with these new tools, you will be able to skillfully navigate any obstacles that stress and anxiety try to throw in your path along your journey.

Surrendering Stress and Anxiety to Divine Guidance

In his book *Jesus and Mastership*, author James Coyle Morgan explains that if we adjust our lives and bodies to be in rhythm with nature, we will live happier and healthier lives.

What this means is that we need to be true to ourselves and follow our divine purpose and plan in this lifetime. When we derail ourselves from this path and become filled with selfishness, or when we focus on creating our lives around only material objects, we are not in tune with the natural forces and energy of Source. This state of being in turn causes confusion and undesirable conditions in our lives. It creates chaos not just within our bodies, but on a larger scale, across the Earth.

As we learned in chapter 2, emotions are a powerful force that can either motivate us to adopt healthier habits or become a barrier to changing our behaviors for the better. Through allowing ourselves to remain burdened with negative emotions, we not only lower our vibrational frequency, where negatives such as illness and dis-ease dwell, but also give our power away to fearful illusions, allowing these to take over our lives and our health.

The great news is that we have free will and the ability to take responsibility for our own thoughts and actions. Often, negative emotions of not being "enough" for ourselves or our loved ones bring up fears and worries in our lives that can develop into chronic stress and anxiety. The best remedy for these feelings is the practice of surrender.

The key to living a stress-free life is to simply let go. Surrender the false need to control every situation. Give this negativity and the illusionary need for control over to Source. Trust that you will be guided to the best possible opportunities for your life. Just as we learned that faith is the key to releasing our fears, you must also trust and have faith in the divine, surrendering the illusion of control in order to heal and be free from stress and anxiety.

Once we have surrendered to Source, one useful tool that can help us learn to access the wisdom available to us via our higher selves is our sixth sense, also known as our third or inner eye, or intuition.

Activate Your Third Eye

Consciousness is the lens through which we experience everything, and as such, it has shaped our understanding of the world around us since the dawn of human existence. But as the Mayans predicted long ago, in 2012 we experienced a crucial time of change in the way we perceive reality. Their prediction of "the end" was simply the end of an era of ego-based consciousness and the beginning of a new age of higher consciousness.

Most of us are aware only of our five physical senses: touch, taste, feeling, sight, and hearing. We have forgotten the most important sense we possess. Rooted in the pineal gland is our sixth sense, also sometimes called the third (or inner) eye. This sense enables us to access our true connection to Source, freeing us form unwanted stress.

We are all beings created by divine energy, and we all have an innate, built-in intuition, or gut instincts. Through the use of our intuition, we have the ability to focus on an outcome of our choice in order to achieve that goal. In connection with our sixth sense, our thoughts and belief systems are the driving force that lead us to experience our truth, purpose, and ultimate healing. Therefore, it is extremely important for us to be conscious of our thought patterns and create positive and loving thoughts instead of negative ones.

Since 2012, when we as a species experienced a large-scale shift in energy, many have surrendered to Source, realizing that the way of the ego—forcing and struggling through life—was no longer working for them. I saw this change manifest when thousands of clients desperate for change poured into my practice and workshops looking for spiritual guidance and healing.

The struggle for survival has been deeply rooted in our experiences on Earth, and this illusion is the work of the ego mind. When we make the choice to live life in the past or the future, buried under the chatter and negative thoughts of the ego mind, we are making the conscious choice to struggle with stress and anxiety.

It is only through surrender and connection to Source that we are sped along our journey, set on a more peaceful path, free from anxiety and worry. Activating and learning to work with your inner eye is what allows you to differentiate between the two paths to achieve your goals that your higher consciousness always offers you: the challenging way of the ego mind, or the easier way of letting go.

The Path Back to Ease of Mind: Surrendering Control

For centuries, we humans have given our control and power to the limiting beliefs of our ego mind. This part of us pushes us to choose the most challenging path. It does this by tricking us into forcing situations to get to our desired goal *now*.

By surrendering the need for control, it is possible to choose the easy path of accepting the flow of energy you draw to yourself from Source through the Law of Attraction, rather than blocking this energy by trying to force your will.

You too can do this. Simply let the energy of your desires flow into your experience freely, trusting in divine timing. When you notice that everything around you seems to be falling apart, the wisest decision is to resist the urge to struggle and force circumstances; rather, open your grip and allow the current situation to clear up, creating room for new, positive energy to move in. Let go of the old static energy to welcome the new experiences.

A simple mantra repeated daily for twenty-one to thirty days may help you reverse the negative energy of control into the more positive energy of allowing things to be as they are in perfect trust. For example, try saying something like "Each day I choose to allow positive opportunities, situations, and people into my life." Remember to be open to allowing this inward flow to come from all directions and sources.

If you are currently experiencing stress, anxiety, or panic

attacks, this is the perfect time for you to tap into and reconnect with your higher consciousness. Be creative in this process and work with your God-given gifts of visualization, as well as your other senses. Allow yourself to feel the sensation of already enjoying that goal, dream, or desire that you hold dear—whatever that may be. Hold your thoughts of your goals and dreams in the present tense, as if you are already experiencing and living them.

Holding positive thoughts and focusing on your goals with unwavering faith will allow you to tap into the unlimited potential and opportunities of the abundant universe. Your determination in doing this exercise repeatedly and as often as possible will help the universe to bring what you desire most to you. Remember what I said earlier: the universe is like a genie in a bottle. It's extremely literal, so whatever energy you focus on and send out is what you will receive back.

It is a common belief among many people that letting go or surrendering equates to losing control over one's life. For those of you who still believe this illusion, I challenge you to practice the techniques in this chapter. Remember the story of my client, Joe. He too was skeptical about this divine truth, but once he gave these techniques a try, he was quick to change his mind. You will be too.

The reality is that you lost control the moment you allowed the illusion of fear, stress, anxiety, and other negative emotions take charge of your life, crippling your mind and body. Just like when starting a new workout routine or diet, you may not see immediate results. But with patience and resolve, practicing surrender every day will yield happier and more positive outcomes in your life, along with drastically reduced stress and anxiety. Remember, the majority, if not all, of the emotions of stress, anxiety, or panic are rooted in fear, and fear is false evidence appearing real.

There is immense potential for healing if you move forward with faith and determination and a willingness to surrender. Let go and let God solve your problems and bless you with the solutions.

The Healing Power of Surrender

I was on vacation when I received a distressed call from the daughter of a soon-to-be client. Three months prior, her mother, Ana, had suffered through a family emergency that had thrown her off balance. This event led to a downward spiral into full-blown stress, anxiety, and panic attacks.

Ana had been hospitalized six times over the past three months due to her symptoms of extreme anxiety, panic attacks, and insomnia. These symptoms were initially a response to the family emergency situation, and they worsened once she began to take the anti-anxiety medications that she had been prescribed. Because Ana was not responding well to traditional methods, the doctor at the hospital recommended hypnotherapy. That's when her family contacted me.

When Ana arrived for her first session, I saw a beautiful middle-aged woman who looked completely hopeless. She had not been able to eat or sleep in more than a month. What's worse, she had completely isolated herself from her family, children, and grandchildren. Before she had become ill, she had been a caretaker for her family, lavishing them with nurturing love and care.

After discussing Ana's options, we decided that the best solution to treat her insomnia, stress, anxiety, and panic attacks would be spiritual guided meditation to bring peace back into her mind and body. Through our sessions, Ana was able to reconnect with herself and Source.

Ultimately, she recognized the truth that nothing can take control of her unless she allows it. With the approval of her doctor, she was able to get off the medications a week after our first session. Once she had reconnected to Source, she was able to go back to her usual loving and joyful self, reunited with and once more surrounded by her loved ones.

As Ana learned through our sessions, one of the greatest characteristics of the subconscious mind is that through sufficient repetition and reinforcement, we are able to learn a new behavior or even create a new belief system. This amazing ability is a big part of what allows us to overcome the illusions of stress and anxiety.

In other words, what you choose to focus on is what you attract to yourself. This is the Law of Attraction at work, but the key in creating this is to do it on a subconscious level. Some of the most powerful tools to release your subconscious limitations and barriers include hypnotherapy, meditation, EFT, and the repetition of mantras and affirmations. These and other tools (some of which you can learn more about if you visit my website, www.journeystoheal.com) will help you release and overcome the subconscious limitations that can create stress. In turn, this will lead you toward a more fulfilled life.

To overcome unwanted stress and anxiety is incredibly simple. Avoid searching for difficult ways to achieve joy and fulfillment.

Instead, find the simplest things that give you joy. Live your life by welcoming more time for laughter, play, and love. In the simplicity of surrender and willful intent rests the true healing potential of mankind.

The stress, worry, and anxiety pushed on by the ego mind need not rule your life. By surrendering the illusion of control to Source, you too can find healing from these negative emotions and their physical manifestations in the body. In the next chapter, our journey of healing continues as we tackle how to release anger and resentment and embrace love and acceptance in their place.

Chapter 5

Healing Anger and Resentment

Spiritual opening is not a withdrawal to some imagined realm or safe cave. It is not a pulling away, but a touching of all the experience of life with wisdom and with a heart of kindness, without any separation.

—Jack Kornfield

The Danger of Holding onto Anger

Sonia had been the victim of sexual abuse when she was a child. When she became an adult, her relationships with men were bogged down with anger, resentment, and mistrust. Every relationship she got into began with fireworks but soon turned into ash. This was in part because her internal ego voice kept pushing Sonia to hurt her partners and leave them before they left her.

She came in to see me with absolutely no hope of ever getting married or having a family for herself, though this was one of her most cherished dreams. Sonia was also angry because she had not been successful in her career choices. She felt lost and disconnected from both the world around her and Source. Trapped in the past, she kept replaying every detail of her past negative experiences. This kept her feeling continually drained on every level: mentally, emotionally, physically, and spiritually.

Due to her childhood trauma, Sonia's root chakra—located below the feminine organs, and the energy center that determines our safety, security, and survival—was completely blocked. As soon as her relationships with men came to the point of intimacy, she found avenues to avoid it. This blockage resulted in high blood pressure, an irregular heartbeat, and sexual dysfunction.

In our sessions, we focused on spiritual meditation, hypnotherapy, and EFT to help Sonia regain a sense of self-acceptance and self-love, and to help her release the baggage of the energy from that particular childhood experience. Learning to let go of anger and resentment was required in order to heal from these emotions, as well as the need to release the underlying fears that caused them. Her healing began, once Sonia committed to more fully loving and accepting herself.

Within a few months, Sonia noticed a significant shift in her energy and sexuality. She felt more connected to her body and no longer feared commitment. Soon after, she manifested the return of a prior love, which developed into a committed and supportive life partner relationship. Today, Sonia and her partner happily share their love with one another and their newborn child.

Commitment to yourself and belief in your own healing leads to freedom from the emotional deadweight of past anger and resentment. Because the mind does not discriminate between what is reality and what is fiction, it gracefully receives and adopts the new, positive information we have committed to giving it. Research shows that when you focus on a specific emotion or thought for at least twenty-one to thirty days, you automatically shift your energy and your experience. As the Law of Attraction states, what you focus on is what you manifest into your reality.

Understanding Anger and Resentment

Anger is a passion of extreme displeasure that leads to the need to punish or hit back whatever or whoever is causing this feeling. But what many fail to realize—much like Sonia before she began her sessions with me—is that the root of all anger and resentment is fear. Buddha said, "Holding on to anger is like grasping a hot coal with the intent of throwing it at someone else; you are the one who gets burned."

In truth, anger is an action created by the ego mind, acting to protect or defend itself. The ego mind is often called the reactive mind, because it reacts to stimuli instead of acting in a calm and or peaceful way to solve problems. Because fear is the root of anger, these two emotions form the two most basic expressions of the ego self.

It's important to deal with and release anger and resentment because, left unchecked, anger can become an explosive and toxic force that destroys not only our own health and well-being, but also the well-being of those around us—essentially, poisoning our relationships with our loved ones. Once we redirect our energy in a positive way, we release the emotion of anger and choose love instead, allowing us to stand up for ourselves, as well as the people and beliefs we care about.

The trick lies in finding balance here, and in order to do that, we must first better understand how anger works.

First, anger causes a specific physiological response in the body. When we get angry, our system releases adrenaline, arousing the body and preparing it for fight or flight. Because of this, when the emotion of anger is stored or suppressed in the system for long periods of time, our approach to life becomes a state of readiness to attack people and situations at all times. This causes us to become a constant hostage to these toxic emotions, which eventually manifest as physical ailments or illness in the body.

Anger and resentment also cause additional negative emotions in us, such as powerlessness and being controlled by others. This in turn only creates more anger, making it easy to get stuck in a vicious cycle of toxicity that becomes increasingly difficult to escape.

The emotion of anger not only causes physical issues, such as high blood pressure and high sugar levels, digestive issues, depression, cancer, and heart problems, but also has damaging effects on our relationships. Anger forces a person into a victim state of mind, isolating him or her from family, friends, and society. Not allowing yourself to feel your anger can lead to equally serious consequences. Suppressed anger destroys the physical body, causing addictions, illness, insomnia, and many other mental and emotional problems.

A perfect example of how not to give in to the fear-based trap of anger and resentment comes from some of the last known words of Jesus, who said, "Forgive them, Father, for they know not what they do." In the midst of His own traumatic experience,

He still refused to allow the illusions of fear and anger to over-power His spirituality. This mindset of grace is something we can all learn from, regardless of our spiritual or religious beliefs.

Nutrition, rest, and exercise all play a big role in managing the energy of anger. The regular use of calcium and magnesium helps calm a person down. In addition, adequate amounts of rest and sleep lower the body's levels of stress and tension from anger.

Only by understanding the emotional and physical causes and consequences of anger can we free ourselves of this fear-based illusion. This healing is made possible by reconnecting with Source, the inner authentic self.

The simple truth is that when we reconnect to our authentic self, we realize the power we have within to overcome any obsta-cle. Anger is an illusion, a static and toxic energy trapped in our bodies. Its presence holds us hostage, denying us healing and joy. When we commit to experiencing joy—our soul's desire—we automatically tap into the energy of releasing and letting go of the illusion of anger.

A body that is filled with the power and energy of love cannot also hold the toxic energy of anger and resentment. Where there is pure love, there is no toxicity, because love vibrates at a very high frequency, whereas negative emotions exist at a very low frequency.

In this chapter, I'll discuss techniques you can use to release feelings of anger and resentment and heal from the damage these negative energies inflict on us. Once you commit to expe-riencing joy and love, you can use their positive force in your life to banish anger and resentment and find your path to true healing.

The Path Back from Anger and Resentment

The essence of the spiritual journey is getting off the wheel of false illusions that appear real to us. As we've learned, these illusions, such as anger and resentment, are fear based. Spiritual development is the key to releasing all anger, because it allows us to tap into the universal truth to see, understand, and release these negative energies and trust that Source has unlimited ways to offer healing and solutions to our problems.

It isn't necessary to struggle to find these solutions or answers. As we've learned in previous chapters, all that is required to access this guidance is to simply make the firm choice to release and let go of our negative energies and let the healing power of Source flow through us.

Becoming attuned to our higher selves leads us to a greater capacity for love and compassion—not only toward others, but also toward ourselves. Meditation is an excellent way to help yourself relax and tap into the power of your subconscious mind to connect with Source. This process will help you to discern the truth in all situations rather than being caught up in illusions that keep us trapped in anger and resentment.

A specific meditation for releasing anger can be found on my website, www.journeystoheal.com. This meditation can help you to relax your sympathetic nervous system, balance your emotions, and become more joyful and less rigid in your thinking.

Affirmations are another powerful way to keep yourself calm and at peace during your daily activities. (Visit my website for examples of affirmations as well.) When faced with the energy of anger, take deep cleansing breaths and exhale slowly and completely. Similarly, when faced with an angry person, choose to remove yourself from the situation rather than diving into it.

Remember: you are responsible only for your own actions and experiences. Blaming someone or something else for your problems only creates more of the toxic energy that is causing harm to you. Taking responsibility for our own mistakes and conquering challenges with a positive attitude helps us solve, dissolve, or let go of what does not work.

Every emotion we create is energy in motion. This means that when we constantly create the energy of anger in our lives, we are inviting still more negative and toxic experiences. This lesson is one that another client of mine, Jane, had yet to learn before she set out on her own journey of healing.

Banishing Anger and Resentment

Jane came to me seeking healing from the anger and resentment she felt toward a family member. As a child, Jane had been mentally, emotionally, and physically tormented by her mother. Her distant memories of her childhood filled her with sadness. She felt trapped by family ties and resented having to visit her mother for any occasion. At the same time, she felt guilty for not being able to heal their relationship.

Over time, this anger and resentment toward her mother began to affect Jane's relationships with her friends. All her life, she had struggled with difficulty in trusting other women. At the point she came to see me, this was beginning to affect her health and career, because her boss and most of the people in her department were female. She had developed cysts in her left breast—precisely where our heart, emotions, and love reside. Additionally, she had high blood pressure and no tolerance or patience for female energy.

Jane was also having trouble sleeping, as many of her dreams contained negative memories of her childhood experiences and fights with her mother. It had gotten so bad that she actively tried to stay awake at night just to avoid these dreams.

During our sessions, Jane vented her deep feelings of anger and resentment, as well as her fears of her mother. Through our shared journey of guided meditations, hypnotherapy, and energy healing, we dissolved the cord attachments between her mother and herself on a mental, emotional, and physical level. By con-scientious practice of the forgiveness exercises I assigned her, she was able to put down any and all details of her memories, venting these out on paper. This helped her release that old, stagnant energy mentally, emotionally, and physically.

One of Jane's sessions was particularly powerful and healing for her. On this day, she envisioned her mother as a large monster and saw herself as a helpless little girl. While we did this exer-cise together, I was shown a vision of her energy expanding, and through that expansion, while she grew taller and more powerful, the vision of her mother as the monster grew smaller and more powerless.

That day, Jane felt the power of her own energy and poten-tial. Within a few months, she was able to set boundaries with her mother and no longer allowed this relationship to dictate her happiness. Now Jane is thriving in her career, as well as in her relationships with her boss, friends, and other women. All of these areas of her life, as well as her health, healed significantly.

And most importantly, she found the courage to address her true emotions with her mother, which helped to facilitate healing in their relationship, too.

After completing our sessions together, Jane was finally able to accept and understand that her mother's own childhood and journey were what dictated her abusive ways, and that this had nothing to do with Jane herself; she was merely the unfortunate recipient of her mother's own anger and resentment. In accepting this, Jane opened herself to one of the divine Source's most powerful healing truths: it is not up to us to try to interfere in others' free will or force them to change.

All we can do is choose to accept ourselves for who and what we are, be conscious observers of our thoughts and feelings, and choose to focus our energies on what makes us healthy, happy, and strong: our connection to Source.

The Power of Owning Our Own Actions and Emotions

Like Jane did, when she first came to see me, you may wonder how you can live a spiritually fulfilled life when you are filled with anger and resentment.

To live mindfully, you must first release the old baggage of anger and resentment toward others.

The secret to letting go of anger and resentment is acceptance. By accepting the past and accepting people for who they are, we honor the fact that they are on their own journey instead of constantly resisting or fighting it. This practice is how we co-create love, the opposite of anger and fear. But this mindful acceptance is not just about accepting others; it also means accepting ourselves and our own actions, and any part we may have played in situations that made us feel angry or resentful.

Taking ownership of your own actions and emotions allows you to operate from your higher consciousness, rather than simply reacting out of anger rooted in fear that comes from the ego mind. This conscious choice on our part allows us to maintain our connection to Source and our authentic selves.

Allow yourself to feel the love and joy of Source energy. Flipping the script on anger and replacing it with love is possible through reestablishing your connection to Source and yourself.

Following this simple yet powerful process of releasing anger and replacing it with joy and love has already transformed thousands of lives. It can only help you.

We can achieve acceptance and inner peace through meditation, yoga, and many other holistic modalities. The key is not to give in to the illusion of anger. Instead, you must connect to what you are truly feeling in your heart in order to see past this illusion. Relax and allow divine miracles of healing to come to you. The spiritual answer to anger is peace, love, and forgiveness of the self and others.

Remember, at the core of all that is, there are only two energies in the world: fear and love. And anger is tied directly to fear.

If you experience anger and resentment on an ongoing basis, stop and think about your experience. What has holding on to the toxic energy of anger and resentment done for you, other than hold you hostage and block you from living life to the fullest?

Which side will you choose to be on from now on? Will it be anger? Or will you choose love, peace, and forgiveness? There is a perfect Bible verse that captures this spiritual task: "Be not quick in your spirit to become angry, for anger lodges in the bosom of fools" (Ecclesiastes 7:9).

Each of us incarnates into a physical body to experience our own journey in this life. While we're on this journey, we are responsible only for our *own* thoughts, feelings, and actions, rather than the thoughts, feelings, or actions of anyone else. Accepting this truth is a big step along the journey to healing, helping us to release anger and resentment and live in the divine light of love and joy.

By reconnecting with Source, embracing responsibility for our own actions and feelings, and refusing to be held accountable for the actions or feelings of others, we can begin to lead happier, healthier lives filled with purpose and beauty.

Now that we've learned how to replace anger and resentment with love and joy, it's time to turn our attention to another toxic emotion that is the enemy of joy: depression. In the next chapter, you'll learn the spiritual root of depression, as well as how to heal this increasingly—and tragically—common illness of the body and mind.

Chapter 6

Healing Depression

We are what we think. All that we are arises with our thoughts. With our thoughts we make the world.

—Gautama Buddha

The Clutches of Depression

Lacie was a particularly intuitive young woman. The minute she first walked through the door, my frequency rose up so high that I felt as if my energetic body was fifty feet tall. When we started discussing her situation, the lights in the room began to flicker. It was clear that our combined energies were attracting supernatural activity in the room. It was equally clear to me that Lacie was a lightworker—a soul who volunteered to be born and help others who have lost their way to heal from the negative effects of fear—trying to spread her wings.

But the situation she was caught in personally was limiting her from experiencing this shift.

For the past several years, Lacie had been taking care of her ill mother, which had resulted in her developing emotions of deep sadness and loss. She was so dedicated that she had left her career and social life behind to make sure her mother was cared for. But after two years of 24/7 caregiving, Lacie felt depressed. Her life had come to revolve only around the four walls of the house and the difficulty of watching her mother suffer.

Because she was such an intuitive and positive soul trapped in the illusion of depression, I recommended an energy healing session combined with spiritual guided meditation. The minute Lacie got on the massage table and we both closed our eyes, I started to experience vividly detailed visions of her journey and purpose in this lifetime.

In the middle of this session, I called on the collective energy to guide her in releasing the illusions of the past and present, to clear her. Just then, I heard bells ringing and saw a gloomy cloud lift from her abdominal and chest area and be replaced with light. My eyes were closed, but I felt her body jerk and heard a deep sigh of relief. She had just released herself from her burdens. I opened my eyes and looked at Lacie's face to see that healing tears had begun to flow.

In that single session, Lacie felt the power of the divine and reconnected to her spiritual journey. One session was all it took for her to remember and reconnect to her path. Afterwards, she was able to let go of her guilt and depression and tap back into her creativity. She found a part-time caregiver for her mother, which allowed her to pursue her dreams and reclaim her social life, without guilt.

Understanding Depression

According to the National Institute of Mental Health, depression affects about 6.7 percent of the US population over the age of eighteen.

Indeed, most of us, at one point in our lives, have experienced the emotion of profound sadness due to loss, struggle, and low self-esteem. But depression has become a generic word in our society. As soon as we feel powerless, hopeless, or helpless, we tend to associate sadness, feelings of loss, or our low self-esteem with the idea that we must be depressed. When we do this, we are in effect blindly giving our power to that illusion.

With many of my clients, our first session begins with them telling me, "I'm depressed." I always ask if they were diagnosed with depression, and the answer is almost always no. This opens us up to the opportunity to explore and get to the core of what it is that disguises itself as emotions of depression, because this word should not be used so lightly. It is also important to remember that sadness, depression, anxiety, and panic attacks are all merely symptoms of something deeper that causes these emotions to surface.

One of the key signs of depression is loss of interest in activities you once enjoyed. Depression commonly occurs with anxiety, panic attacks, phobias, and in some cases eating disorders. It affects the release of serotonin and norepinephrine in the brain, which influence moods and discomfort in the physical body.

Many sufferers of depression go from doctor to doctor seeking treatment for their physical symptoms when, in fact, they should look into mental and emotional healing. By giving in to and embracing the word *depression* (as with any other illness or diagnosis), you simply open your arms and surrender to that illusion, forgetting that you are a spiritual being and that nothing or no one can take your power unless you give it up. Why speak through labels? Labeling limits our spiritual journey. As Buddha said, "Rule your mind or it will rule you."

When we get caught up in the low energy of labels, we cease operating as our higher selves.

We have all experienced symptoms of deep sadness or discontent at one point in our lives. The key is not to give in to the illusion of suppressed feelings that disguise themselves as depression or begin to live our lives through it. Instead, you must reconnect with your spiritual center in order to find true healing from the illusion of depression.

In this chapter, I'll discuss how to cast off the label of depression and reconnect with your infinite capacity for divine healing through Source and through the power of spiritual release.

Identifying Depression

What can we do to overcome and heal from depression? First, you must determine if your symptoms are actually due to depression, and if so, determine the cause of it. The cause of depression may be both emotional and physical, due to inadequate diet, lack of exercise, emotional attachments to past traumatic events, and not enough rest or sleep.

An appropriate first step would be to make sure you're taking care of yourself mentally and physically. Are you getting enough rest, healthy food, and exercise, and allowing yourself the time you need to recharge your mind? Are you surrounding yourself with positive people who lift you up? Are you engaging socially with friends and family, to feed your spirit?

It's also a good idea to consult with your physician or psychotherapist. If your therapist determines that you are not clinically depressed, seek alternative therapeutic ways such as meditation, hypnotherapy, or aromatherapy and remember that by reconnecting with your authentic divine self you can heal any physical problem, including one that causes—or is caused by—depression.

Research shows that regular meditation or other activities help thicken the brain cortex, which helps guard against depression. MRI scans reveal thicker cortices in individuals who placed importance on spirituality.

All illness, be it mental, emotional, or physical, begins in the mind. Remember that you are not a part of any label or diagnosis, and it is not a part of you. The following client story demonstrates the importance of not giving in to labels.

The Path Back from Depression

When Evette came in for her first session, she brought all her prescription medications with her. My first impression was that a twenty-four-year-old should never be taking so many pills. She was taking medication for anxiety, depression, panic attacks, and stress and had recently been prescribed still more medications to combat the physical symptoms she was having in response to all the anxiety and depression meds she was already taking.

These medications were causing insomnia, addiction to the medication, high blood pressure, and an uncontrollable weight gain, among other issues. When I first looked into her eyes, Evette couldn't stay still. She was drowsy and had a difficult time putting her thoughts together.

Hypnotherapy was her last resort. She had been to traditional therapy, but it hadn't yielded results. So her current doctor had recommended hypnotherapy, which, if successful, would allow her to slowly be weaned off the meds with her doctor's approval. Her underlying condition and the reason for all the medications was that she despised her job and was in an emotionally abusive relationship.

Evette felt lost, trapped, hopeless, and worthless.

After I spoke with Evette to learn about what was going on in her life, we determined that the best solution was to work together using hypnotherapy techniques to rebuild her confidence, self-esteem, and self-love.

Our mission was to reprogram her subconscious and disconnect the illusions of negative thoughts that kept playing and replaying in her mind. Many of these were created by her abusive relationship with her significant other. EFT was another tool that I introduced in our sessions, to help her release stagnant energy and accept herself as the spiritual, powerful, and beautiful soul that she is.

In our hypnotherapy and spiritual meditation sessions, I applied essential oils directly to her body to help raise her frequency. During this process, I guided her to see the truth of who she is and what she represents and, most importantly, to recognize her self-worth. In order to heal, Evette needed to learn that she is worthy of happiness, joy, love, and peace. Each week, I gave her the recording of our session and assigned her exercises and mantras to use to free her mind, body, and spirit from the illusions that were making her sick.

After four months of working together, and under the recommendation of her doctor, Evette was able to get off of her medications. Part of her healing process involved being able to release her relationship to the universe. The relationship quickly dissolved away, because it was not for her highest good or the highest good of her partner. But the most amazing shift occurred when she found a new career opportunity, which was closer to her career goals and came with higher pay than the "job" she'd felt stuck in for so long.

By the six-month mark, she had lost almost all the extra weight she'd been carrying and started a new life for herself. Evette changed her diet, began exercising, and attracted new, positive people and friends who helped her build a joyful social life. She is the perfect example of our inner power when we are determined to achieve what we desire in life.

The Healing Power of Spiritual Release

No illusion is ever too big for divinity. As Evette did, surrender all your grief and burdens to Source and, through spiritual meditations, hypnotherapy, and other holistic modalities, you too can regain your innate power of healing.

One of the key aspects of achieving spiritual well-being is learning to overwrite your old, negative beliefs with positive ones. When you look closer into your heart, you will see that there is always hope, love, and positivity there. As we've learned in previous chapters, fear or depression is created by the ego mind—not by the heart or the spirit. Creating simple positive mantras for yourself or working with the ones you can find at my website (www.journeystoheal.com) can help you overwrite any tormenting thoughts and fears that come from the ego. Remember, repetition is the most powerful tool our mind can work with to overwrite negative thought patterns.

In surrendering her feelings of guilt and sadness to Source, Evette was able to free herself from the illusion of being depressed and launch herself on a personal journey of spiritual reconnection. This led not only to healing her troubling physical, mental, and emotional symptoms, but also to releasing stagnant and toxic relationships and situations that were holding her back from finding true fulfillment.

In Buddhism, depression is approached from a different viewpoint than it is in Western psychology. Buddhists see depression as an underlying selfishness/egotism. They also believe that karma or past lives can have a role in us feeling depressed in this lifetime. They believe that by opening our minds and hearts to compassion and loving kindness, we can overcome this illusion. This path leads to a journey of self-acceptance, self-confidence, and satisfaction with life and ourselves.

Genuinely wishing and radiating happiness for ourselves and others shifts our minds to dramatically change our experiences. By changing our minds and thoughts, we have the power to change our moods and lives.

Speaking of karma, for some clients, their negative illusions are rooted not in the troubles of this life, but in energies they have carried over from their past-life experiences. In the next chapter, we'll learn more about past-life energies and how to heal from their effects using regression therapy.

Chapter 7

Healing Past Life Attachments

To be able to look back upon one's past life with satisfaction is to live twice.

—*Lord Acton*

Relationship Remedy

During my first consultation with Lisa, the events of her past sounded like something out of a movie. She told me, although both she and her partner continued to cause each other considerable emotional and mental anguish, it seemed there was no way out. In the midst of all that pain, they each felt they could not live a single day without the other. It was evident to me that this was a connection from their past lives, and that there was unfinished business between them.

Based on the details of Lisa's story, I decided that past-life regression therapy would be the best therapeutic approach for her case. We proceeded to the recliner to begin, and as I guided her, Lisa sunk deeper into her subconscious awareness to access the memories from her past lives that may have been troubling her in the present. Very quickly, she was able to access memories of a previous life in France sometime around the 1760s.

She saw herself wearing an ornate gown and standing in a beautiful and luxurious garden. As she walked through this garden, she was greeted by a handsome male in his thirties, whom she recognized as the soul of her current partner.

She described their love affair in that past life in France as something out of a fairytale. And yet her former self knew that their relationship couldn't last: she was the daughter of a well-respected and rich businessman, and the man she loved was her family's servant. Soon her vision switched to the moment where all of her pain and suffering began. She described the two of them standing near a lake, a place they would often meet in secret in that lifetime, but with one twist: this time he was not waiting there for her.

As she approached the lake, she noticed something strange in the water. When she looked closer, she saw her lover's eyes staring back at her, filled with terror. He was dead—drowned, because her father had found out about their love affair.

In the present moment of our session, tears rolled down Lisa's face. Recalling this painful memory of heartbreak, loss, and betrayal was an agony, but the vision quickly changed to a scene later in that lifetime when she was in so much pain that she ended up going to the same lake and taking her own life with a knife to her heart.

Given their turbulent relationship in the present time, it was evident that both her soul and her partner's had carried this tragic experience from their past lives into this lifetime. It was time to clear away this pain so that they might each begin anew.

The first step in healing Lisa's past life attachment and pain was to start while she was still in that deep subconscious state of mind. We healed this memory through the use of suggestions that helped her realize this pain belonged to the past and that she needed to release and let go of the emotions she felt in the present.

While I was giving her the suggestions to release and let go of these feelings from her previous life, Lisa's body began to shake. The process of releasing the pain of these memories appeared to be happening on a deep cellular level. She shook and cried, and within minutes, all of that suddenly stopped. Lisa took a deep breath and went into a peaceful state.

It was at that moment that she finally let go of the lingering pain of that tragic past memory.

Shortly after our session, Lisa reported that all her fears about losing her partner and the lingering, subconscious thoughts and feelings of not being able to live without him had dissipated. Once these memories were accessed and healed and the cords to that lifetime were dissolved, their relationship started to heal, and they became inseparable in a positive way. Finally, they were able to enjoy just being together, a long-overdue cause for much joy in both of their lives.

Understanding Past Life Attachments

Past-life regression therapy is used to resolve experiences from past lives that continue to block our progress and happiness in the current lifetime. This is sometimes needed when the subconscious mind carries forward experiences, attitudes, behaviors, and relationships from prior lives into the current life. Often, traumatic experiences such as violence or the loss of a loved one or a relationship are left unresolved and in desperate need of healing.

Past-life situations can also be activated by events in your current life without your conscious awareness. Because these problems are rooted deep in the subconscious, where they remain difficult to access, this may result in additional trauma in the current life. This can create an energy block that cannot be resolved, no matter how much effort is put into healing the problem—not until the stagnant energy of the problematic past-life memories has been released and cleared away.

The process of past-life regression therapy mentally takes you back to the time and place where the original trauma, situation, or issue occurred. This is achieved through a deep state of relaxation such as guided imagery or hypnosis, allowing you to access past-life memories from your subconscious. By accessing and bringing these memories to conscious awareness, you can then resolve the trauma or issue and release that energy block that was keeping you stuck.

When you re-experience those key events from past lives and process them during the therapy session, the impact enables you to bring closure to those events almost instantly, thus allowing you to move forward more freely. This type of therapy is typically used to overcome issues that are not related to experiences in your current life. It is also extremely useful for those who want to improve their experience in the present lifetime or increase their confidence.

Past-life regression therapy can also heal psychological and physical trauma such as headaches, allergies, asthma, ulcers, and arthritis. In some cases, it even helps eliminate tumors in the body caused by cancer.

Another benefit of this technique is that you're not limited to recalling only negative memories from past lives. You can also use this kind of therapy to access positive experiences from your prior lifetimes, such as strengths, wisdom, accomplishments, and even skills. These positive memories can also stimulate healing and personal growth by helping you tap into the inner wisdom you have accumulated from your past lives.

In this chapter, I'll show you how you too can heal yourself from the pain of past-life attachments through regression therapy. Once you learn to release the pain of traumatic memories from previous lifetimes, you'll be free to more fully embrace your path to healing and fulfillment in this lifetime.

My Experience with Past-Life Regression Therapy

Before I could begin to offer past-life regression therapy to my clients, I first had to resolve my own religious fears about reincarnation. When I was first offered classes on this powerful technique at my hypnotherapy school, I was extremely excited, but at the same time, I had many questions and fears. For some time, these kept coming up and trying to hold me back from learning this powerful technique for healing. This was the chatter of my ego mind at work.

Ultimately, the one thing that kept me moving forward with this leg of my journey was my faith and trust in Source. My journey had already been one of healing through my connection to my authentic, higher self. If my higher self had put me on this path and brought this opportunity my way, then I had to trust that it was safe to try this new path to healing. I was determined not to let negative energy tied to my fear-based religious upbringing hold me back.

In order to truly understand this process, I first needed to experience past-life regression myself. I sensed that this might be helpful, because many situations in my current lifetime didn't make sense. Over time, I personally experienced more than ten past-life regression sessions. In each one, I saw and healed an average of between five to ten lives, and soon one common theme became apparent through all of them: most of my past lives ended in tragedy, because I was frequently accused of being a witch due to my spiritual gifts.

My most tragic past-life recall, and the one that was hardest to process and release, was one in which I was a teenage girl with many healing talents and gifts. One day, I had gone into the woods to gather plants to prepare medicine for a neighbor. But when I exchanged the medicine for money, I was captured by a group of people bent on persecuting witches.

During the regression session, I felt my physical body in the present time start to shiver, and I couldn't understand where I was or what was happening. As I patiently asked questions to figure out where I was, I began to see and feel myself in a small box that was thrown into the ocean. In terror, I watched my entire family from that lifetime sobbing, distraught over what was happening to me, but unable to help.

As uncomfortable as this memory was, I recognized some

familiar souls in it. I realized that my mother in that lifetime is my daughter now, and my little brother from that time is now my son.

In the present moment, my body continued to shiver. I couldn't control this, so I trusted that it was necessary and allowed the process to continue until, finally, I released this traumatic memory on a cellular level.

The best part about this process for me was that, after this particular session and with each successive regression, I was able to release my fears of losing loved ones and the discomfort of accepting money for my gifts. By clearing up this stagnant energy of past-life attachments, I was no longer afraid to pursue a course in past-life regression therapy.

Using this powerful therapeutic technique, many of my clients have overcome illnesses, relationship problems, and long-standing fears in their current lives that are rooted in issues from their past lives. Others have also overcome the fear of dying by gaining awareness that our spirits live on.

The most exhilarating component to past life regression is that we are not limited to only experiencing past lives, our subconscious has the ability to also access and explore lives in between, future lifetimes, channel and receive crucial life changing information from the higher self, and even channel loved ones that have crossed over.

In some past-life regression sessions, spirits bring forth healing messages to help clients overcome their fears. These sessions in particular stand out as being particularly rewarding.

Guidance from Spirit

When Janet walked in for her first session, her appearance was stylish and collected, her short hair beautifully colored and combed back. But her eyes told a different story, holding tremendous fear, anxiety, and worry.

When she wrote down her list of what she wanted to work on, we determined that she needed past-life regression therapy to release baggage from her past. We had discussed the possibility of spirits showing up in our sessions before we began, and Janet was open to receiving this kind of help. Sure enough, starting from her first session, a spirit was present to guide her healing journey. This spirit's powerful presence truly helped Janet to overcome the burdens she still shouldered that were rooted in her past-life experiences.

From the first moment that this spirit showed up, I could feel the tremendous love energy it was bringing through—to the extent that at one point, Janet and I were both in tears. The spirit gave specific details of items owned by Janet's family that she was instructed to investigate after our session. We were told that these items held clues that would help us to understand who the spirit was.

The following session, Janet returned, anxious to give me the details of what she had found. She sat down, an expression of childlike excitement on her face, and told me that when she had told her mother about what the spirit had said, her mother had smiled. The spirit was her mother's favorite aunt, who had taken care of her and given her unconditional love when she was a little girl.

As we continued with our sessions, Janet's great-aunt continued to provide powerful guidance, leading us in the right direction and helping Janet to heal and grow closer to Source. After six sessions, Janet was able to open to universal love and dissolve her illusions, which positively affected not only her own life, but her mother's and daughter's lives as well. Janet's health began to take a positive turn, and her business also began to flourish. Many positive opportunities began to show up for her family soon after.

The Healing Power of Releasing Past-Life Attachments

Past-life regression is considered to be a holistic therapy because it works with your mind, body, spirit, and, most importantly, your emotions. Because it treats the whole person, it is an excellent tool to use in healing everything from relationship issues to chronic illnesses, phobias, addictions, sexual dysfunction, nightmares, fear of death, and many other obstacles in our lives.

Unlike cognitive therapy, which is done on a conscious and intellectual level of the mind and, as such, can take years to complete, this type of therapy can be done relatively quickly. This means it can be of tremendous use in speeding up the healing process.

Often clients are also able to access the life they live *between* lives, which enables the individual to connect with his or her authentic spiritual self. This connection to our higher selves allows for the discovery and understanding on a much deeper level that the soul is immortal. When clients tap into this energy and the reenactment of a previous death experience, they also tap into the peace that followed.

This kind of recall is enlightening and has the power to dissolve away the fear of death. As such, this powerful technique has the potential to transform your life. In the process, you may unlock hidden talents and reveal the purpose for which you incarnated in this lifetime. Past-life regression therapy can also help you overcome any limiting or fear-based religious beliefs that continue to hold you back. You do not need to believe in reincarnation to achieve the healing powers of this wonderful therapeutic technique.

The inner peace, healing, and self-acceptance achieved through past-life regression sessions help us to understand the deeper meaning that collectively underlies our many lifetimes. Ultimately, this awareness is a powerful tool that helps you to see the truth of who you are as a spiritual being, rather than allowing yourself to be drawn in by the earthly illusions of the ego mind and all the pain, suffering, and dis-ease that they bring.

Now you've learned another powerful tool to help you travel the path to spiritual fulfillment and ultimate healing through Source, free of the emotional and physical burdens we sometimes carry with us from previous lifetimes. In the next chapter, we'll explore another burden many of us face: the profound sense of emptiness that leads us to struggle with all manner of addictions.

Chapter 8

Healing Addiction

Our greatest weakness lies in giving up. The most certain way to succeed is always to try just one more time.
—*Thomas A. Edison*

Filling the Emptiness

When Alice first called me to set up an appointment, her voice was filled with desperation as she described a lifelong pattern of addiction to food and unhealthy relationships. As a child, she had been the victim of emotional abuse. Her father had been very critical of her, continually undermining Alice and calling her cruel names. She grew up believing that the things he told her were true: that she was nothing, that she was stupid, and that she was unworthy of love.

While still operating out of this adopted illusory belief she had learned from her father, as an adult, Alice developed a pattern of drawing emotionally abusive men into her life. Another problem she faced as an adult stemmed from something she had learned from her mother. Starting in Alice's childhood, her mother had taught Alice to treat food as a way to provide comfort and a false sense of safety and security to insulate herself against her father's drunken and unkind ways.

As an adult, this translated into a binge-eating habit, as Alice used food to temporarily numb the discomfort and pain she felt in her mind and heart. At one point, she gained more than forty pounds due to her binge eating. Because of the emptiness and mistrust she felt inside, she turned away from everyone around her, as well as from herself and from Source.

In addition to her growing weight gain, Alice found herself in an abusive relationship. Meanwhile, her career and finances began to go downhill as well, due to her volatile emotional state. She reached a point where she began having difficulty expressing her true thoughts and emotions, and continually felt like a door-mat—both within her family and in the workplace. Alice was caught in an increasingly fast-moving downward spiral, and she couldn't find her way out of it.

The solution to Alice's problem was to achieve spiritual whole-ness, through strengthening her sense of self-love, confidence, and trust in herself and Source. We accomplished this using a combination of hypnotherapy, spiritual healing techniques and exercises, EFT, and meditation.

Through the use of hypnotherapy suggestions, Alice was finally able to release all the toxic childhood fears and anger she still held toward her father. She learned to forgive him and under-stand that what he had done to her was merely a result of his own inner pain. Understanding that his pain had caused him to lash out and create more pain instead of giving his child the love that she deserved was an important first step. Next, EFT helped Alice to accept and love herself for who she is, and the meditation I taught her helped her to remain spiritually centered on a daily basis.

The combination of these therapies allowed Alice to reconnect to what was missing in her life: her connection to her highest and most authentic self. Once this connection was reestablished and she felt whole again, she no longer felt the sense of emptiness that had driven her to give in to the illusion of addiction. After our sessions, Alice lost the extra weight she had gained and finally attracted a partner who treats her with the love and respect that she deserves.

Understanding Addiction

Like the other illusions we've learned about, addiction is born out of disconnection from our authentic selves. What's uniquely dangerous about the illusion of addiction, though, is that it's particularly seductive. By its nature, it forces the individual to get caught up in its sway to put all of his or her focus and energy into that illusion.

This in turn leads to detachment and disconnection from the present moment and from the authentic self, which isolates the individual and sinks him or her only deeper into the darkness of the illusion. Because this creates a cyclical pattern of self-hate, anger, resentment, and feelings of unworthiness, the trap of addiction can seem impossible to escape once you're caught in it. But this is simply not true. Like any other illusion, addiction can be healed through reconnecting to Source energy, your inner power.

It's important to understand that addiction is not always the real problem of the addicted individual. Because love is the ultimate goal of our higher selves, each of us incarnates into the world and into our physical bodies in order to physically experience the giving and receiving of love. But sometimes, traumatic experiences during childhood or other points in our lives force us to turn to dangerous substances or behaviors to numb the pain that we feel.

Addictions are the direct outcome of feelings of emptiness that result from disconnection to our higher selves and the divine love of Source. They are our attempt to fill that emptiness with something else—whatever is handy that makes us forget the pain of that disconnection, even if that substance or behavior does physical, mental, and emotional damage to us.

For this reason, the first step to overcoming addiction is to go within. We must commit to investing the time and effort needed to face whatever suppressed emotions and memories of the past are standing in the way of our ability to heal and move past our addictions. Only by shining the light of the truth on the darkest and most difficult emotions that are trapped within us can we heal from this illusion. Just as we nourish our bodies with food on a daily basis, the soul requires its own food, to recharge and nourish itself. By bringing these emotions to the surface and experiencing them without judgment in a therapeutic setting, we can release this energy on a cellular level.

When you go within to connect to Source and your authentic self, you tap into its eternal, unlimited love and support. This connection then becomes the catalyst to your healing. In this chapter, I'll show you how to reconnect with your authentic self to heal from your addictions by achieving spiritual wellness and wholeness. I'll share with you some of what I've learned about how addiction works, as well as another client story that illustrates the power of spiritual connection in healing the illusory sense of emptiness that lies at the root of addiction.

Addiction and Astrology

While doing research on why some people unknowingly choose to give their power to addictions, I came across some astounding information connected to astrology. Individuals who have a strong Neptune or Pisces energy in their chart often unintentionally become victims of addiction. This is because Neptune rules addictions to alcohol, drugs, suffering, and deception.

The energy of Neptune creates this illusion because it plays a major role in our belief systems. This energy directs the questions we pose regarding what our purpose is on Earth and what Source represents. Although in some cases, people end up losing their lives to their addictions, in other cases, walking a path through and ultimately out of the illusion of addiction inadvertently leads to surrendering to Source and a deepened and renewed sense of spiritual connection. When an individual hits rock bottom and still survives, then he or she has nowhere else to go but up.

Surprisingly, Neptune also has the ability to offer us the energy of enlightenment. This leads us to become curious and ask questions intended to gain a greater understanding of how to reconnect to our hearts. Ultimately, our souls are hungry for love, which is easily fulfilled by spiritual connection.

Another important aspect of addiction also directed through Neptune's energy is the addiction to mental suffering. Many experience this, yet they do not recognize what it is, much less how to overcome it.

How can you recognize if you are addicted to mental suffering? Take a closer look at your own life. Do you believe you lack control over your thoughts and emotions? Do you spend most of your time dwelling on all the negatives in your life from past and present? Are you constantly worried about the future? Do you blame yourself and others for your own suffering and attract drama in your life? Are you stuck in negative patterns, and do you have a hard time letting go of the past?

If you answered yes to any of those questions, then you, like so many others, are addicted to mental suffering. But you too can heal yourself of the illusion of this addiction. The following story shows how one client took charge and overcame the challenges of addiction by achieving awakening through spiritual reconnection.

Healing from Addiction

Patrick was a thirty-eight-year-old man addicted to emotional suffering. When he arrived for our first session, his body language betrayed his tortured emotional state. He was hunched over, and his eyes were filled with despair.

For most of his life, he had been addicted not only to emotional suffering, but also to prescription drugs. We traced the root of this problem to a tragedy from his youth: he lost his father when he was just a teenager. After Patrick's father died, his mother had to work three jobs to provide for their family, and even then, they lived a limited lifestyle. Patrick was the oldest of four children, and he had to grow up very quickly in order to act as a father figure for his younger siblings.

By the time he was an adult, Patrick's addictions were the only way he could numb the pain of his memories of those difficult years.

When he first began his sessions with me, Patrick's addictions had already taken a toll on his physical body, as well as his life. He had high blood pressure, digestion issues, and insomnia, and he was experiencing aches and pains in his abdomen. Because of the emptiness he felt inside, he was unable to hold on to committed love relationships, and his goals of being his own boss were a distant dream.

In order to help him release the energy of his childhood memories, I introduced Patrick to hypnotherapy to allow him to acknowledge his painful memories and effectively "zap" them to destroy and dissolve their energy. We also worked with energy healing and aromatherapy, which allowed his physical body to relax and move into a healing space.

This combined approach of hypnotherapy and energy healing helped Patrick to release his emotional suffering, resulting in stabilizing his blood pressure, regulating his digestive system, overcoming his insomnia, and releasing the emotionally based aches and pains from his body.

When I first introduced the idea that 70 percent of our physical pain is emotionally connected, he smiled in disbelief. But after we completed his therapy, Patrick happily admitted that he now firmly believes that most of his physical pain had indeed been connected to his emotional state.

Armed with this new knowledge, Patrick used the power of his mind—through positive affirmations—to change his energy. Today, Patrick is living on the East Coast with his girlfriend.

Not only is he succeeding in his love life, but he was finally able to embark upon his lifelong dream of having his own computer repair business. His life is now thriving and balanced in all areas.

The Healing Power of Spiritual Wholeness

It is important to understand that the path to overcoming any type of addiction, no matter how deep the individual is into it, is through reconnection to our higher self. Because we make every choice in life through our own free will, our higher self never forces us into enlightenment and healing. Instead, it patiently shows us the truth until we are ready to make the changes we need to move forward.

You are a spiritual being having a human experience; the human experience is not greater or more powerful than you. No matter how challenging your circumstances may seem, or how much you have suffered in the past, as long as you commit yourself to the change you desire, then nothing can stop you.

One of the most profound ways to overcome and recover from addiction is to be of service to others. Giving back helps us to regain a sense of self-love and worth. It also gives us the purpose, hope, and goals needed to live life to our full potential. Through acts of service, we deepen our connection with others, creating the catalytic energy of giving and receiving of love that is the ultimate truth and goal of every soul. This creates feelings of good health and well-being that manifest into our physical, day-to-day lives.

The answer to healing addictions is reconnecting with the higher self to fill the illusion of emptiness inside of us with something real. All the wealth, beauty, power, fame, or success in the world cannot possibly replace the fulfillment and satisfaction you feel when you are connected to your heart and truth.

Committing to regular spiritual practice of meditation is a powerful tool that allows you to find meaning and purpose in your life. Addictions cause fear and can lead to a downward spiral, but by reconnecting with yourself, you can put an end to ego mind chatter and begin to feel centered, mindful, and present in your own life.

Now that we've learned how to cast off the illusion of addiction and fill the emptiness in our hearts with divine love and light, let's continue onward in our journey of healing. In the next chapter, we'll learn how the inability to forgive can block our spiritual progress, as well as how to release and heal from the harm caused by others through reconnecting to the divine energy.

Chapter 9

Healing Unforgiveness

By bringing about a change in our outlook toward things and events, all phenomena can become sources of happiness.

—*Dalai Lama*

Holding on to Unforgiveness

Jack was in his early twenties when he contacted me seeking help to release the unforgiveness he felt toward his father.

Growing up, he was one of four children and the second-born son. All his life, his father had been extremely critical and judgmental of his actions. Over the years, he learned to avoid his father and basically raised himself without a mentor or guide to help him learn right from wrong. As an adult, he felt like a child trapped in a grown-up body, desperately seeking his father's love, attention, and approval. Eventually, he noticed that the unforgiveness he was holding toward his father was negatively affecting his relationship with his friends and his career.

Because his case involved emotions that existed on the subconscious level of the mind, we quickly dove into our therapy sessions. Shortly after, Jack began to understand and distance himself from his father's journey, coming to see that his father's interpretation of parenting was through tough love. His dad was merely acting based on the way his own father had raised him, similarly raising Jack to be "a tough guy."

Ultimately, Jack had to accept that his father's actions had nothing to do with him; they were merely an expression of the internal turmoil his father felt and did not know how to free himself from. Through hypnotherapy and spiritual guided meditation, Jack was able to release the unforgiveness he was holding toward his father. He rebuilt his confidence, and learned to exercise self-love and gratitude each day of his life.

Soon after our sessions, he went back to school to finish his degree. Today, Jack is thriving in his career, his love life, and his relationships with his friends.

Understanding the Inability to Forgive

Forgiveness is one of the most important pieces of the puzzle to spiritual growth and enlightenment.

Forgiveness does not mean that you deny or forget the other person's actions or words. Instead, it means separating the person from his or her actions. This means that you can forgive someone without excusing his or her actions. In practical terms, forgiveness helps you heal and move forward with your life, while unforgiveness keeps you stuck in that toxic energy, which negatively affects all areas of your life, from love to career, health, and finances. That toxic energy lowers your frequency and throws your energy off balance, wreaking havoc on all areas of your life.

It's also important to understand that the decision to forgive someone's actions or words must come genuinely. Allowing ourselves to forgive one another—or even ourselves—allows us to heal, releasing the shackles that hold us down. Only when we forgive can we begin to focus on the love, joy, and happiness that surround us. The illusion of unforgiveness is a creeping gloom that prevents us from seeing the true beauty that life has to offer.

The path you choose determines your happiness and experiences. There is not a human being in the world who has not been hurt by the actions or words of another. It's possible that, when you were growing up, your parents and friends criticized or judged you, or that as an adult, your significant other cheated on you. These wounds caused by the words or actions of others can leave you with lasting feelings of anger, bitterness, or even a desire for revenge.

The unfortunate truth is that those who do not forgive are the ones who pay the price. Dwelling on past hurts only creates more problems for you, because eventually that anger and sadness turn into resentment and hostility toward everyone around you. Left unchecked, this negative behavior soon takes over your entire life. You begin to bring anger and bitterness into every relationship. Your life becomes so wrapped up in the negative that you can no longer enjoy being in the present moment, the company of those around you, or life in general.

If you overwhelm yourself with the negative energy of unforgiveness over the years, it not only consumes your life and happiness, but also causes physical illness. The mind and the body begin to crumble under all that toxic negative energy. This state of chronic unforgiveness pushes you further away from your loved ones. Most importantly, you lose the connection with your authentic self and spiritual purpose.

In this chapter, I'll discuss how to release the pain of old wounds and embrace the healing power of true forgiveness. Once you let go of the toxic energy of unforgiveness, you'll find that you're more open to giving and receiving the love and joy that life has to offer.

A Cry for Help

A woman in her mid-thirties, Maria, walked into my office desperate to free herself from the dangerous thoughts and feelings of unforgiveness she had been experiencing for many months.

She came in dressed like a teenage girl, wearing a simple white shirt, blue jeans, and her hair tightly tied into a ponytail. During the cognitive portion of our session, she mentioned feeling enveloped in love and hope for change. I discovered that her challenge was that she had been a part of a successful business partnership for more than a decade, but she felt that she was living in the shadow of her partner.

Maria felt as if her entire life was a dream and that she was not really a part of it. This had begun to take a huge toll on her health and her relationship with her partner. She developed asthma, insomnia, high blood pressure, and an addiction to emotional eating. Through all of this, she was filled with hate, anger, and resentment.

Because her issues were present on all levels—mental, emotional, spiritual, and physical—I recommended hypnotherapy, past-life regression therapy, and energy healing for our sessions together. During one of her past-life regression therapy sessions, we discovered multiple lives she had lived with the soul of her current business partner where she had been chained up, tortured, and kept as hostage. Following this discovery, Maria found forgiveness within herself and released the emotional shackles that had kept her a hostage in this relationship.

As we continued to work together on a weekly basis, I noticed that she began to come out of her shell more and more. This was possible because, through our sessions, Maria learned the importance of self-love, self-esteem, finding her voice, and having the courage to speak up.

Soon, her energy shifted and her chakras began to open and balance, until Maria was in such deep surrender mode that after each session, the rapid results of her healing were plainly evident. Each week, she shed another layer of illusion created by the ego. Her anger, resentment, hate, and fears dissipated, while her self-esteem and confidence improved, allowing her inner beauty to shine through.

At this point, Maria's company Christmas party was fast approaching, and for the first time, she was excited to show the true beauty of who she was. At our follow-up session after the party, she cried tears of joy as she shared her experience with me. Whereas in the past, she had dreaded having to speak onstage at this annual event, for the first time, she'd felt totally confident and at ease on that stage.

The following months brought more drastic and wonderful changes into her life. She started to shed the extra pounds she had gained and changed her entire outlook on her life, health, and eating habits. Because of her determination to achieve forgiveness and reconnect with her highest self, Maria now lives a life filled with wonderful opportunities and loving relationships, and she continually succeeds in her business ventures.

The Healing Power of Forgiveness

The key to surrendering unforgiveness is taking responsibility in changing what no longer works in your life. Don't waste your energy on judging how and what others say or do. It's a lot easier to see the wrongdoing of others than to take a hard look at yourself. Remember: it's not your responsibility to interfere in others' free will or to try to change their ways. You are responsible only for your own thoughts, feelings, and actions.

Releasing the energy of unforgiveness frees your mind, body, and spirit. When you feel you are ready to forgive, stop trying to control the situation or seeing yourself as the victim. Instead, surrender to Source and release those toxic emotions for the sake of your own healing.

When you forgive yourself or those who have hurt you in the past, you are exercising your spirituality. As a direct result, you will begin to experience more peace, hope, gratitude, and joy in your life. Most importantly, forgiveness helps you heal on all levels: mental, emotional, and physical. Letting go of the bitter negative energy of old hurts and wounds helps you have more loving relationships, increases your spiritual connection to yourself, dissolving away stress, anxiety, and hostility from your life.

If you find it challenging to forgive yourself or someone else, one of the techniques that can help you release or vent is to journal. Vent out every little detail about the situation and remember to be ready to burn it afterward. Burning your words after you purge them from your mind is a good way to get rid of that energy and move forward.

Another way to heal unforgiveness is to find a wise and compassionate person, such as a spiritual counselor, and let him or her guide you toward healing. One of the most effective—and one of my favorite—ways to overcome this toxic energy is to use guided meditation, because this process allows you to heal on a subconscious level. If you visit my website at www.journeystoheal.com, you will find mantras, affirmations, guided meditation CD's and several exercises that will lead you to the freedom of forgiveness.

Use these tools and techniques to reconnect with your infinite self and unburden yourself from the dark cloud of unforgiveness, and soon you will be able to see the true beauty of the world around you.

Now that you've learned the benefits of embracing forgiveness and releasing the toxic energy of holding on to past hurts, it's time to take the last step on our journey of healing: learning about the mind-body-spirit connection, and how you can take advantage of the incredibly intricate system that makes up who you are.

In the next chapter, I'll discuss the individual needs of the mind, body, and spirit, as well as cover in brief a variety of healing techniques and modalities that can offer you relief from whatever physical, mental, or emotional suffering you may be experiencing. Our miraculous journey toward healing is drawing closer to its end point: a future in which you are free to experience joy, happiness, good health, and success in all areas of your life.

Chapter 10

Solutions for the Body, Mind, and Spirit

The body heals with play, the mind heals with laughter, and the spirit heals with joy.

—Proverb

The Body-Mind-Spirit Connection

While they may seem like separate parts of us, in truth, the mind, body, and spirit function as one unit.

You have probably experienced this unity of body, mind, and spirit—maybe more than you realize. Think about a time in your life when you experienced a physical response in your body due to your mental or emotional state. Perhaps you get headaches or stomachaches from stress. Similarly, nearly everyone is familiar with the way hunger or physical fatigue can slow down one's mental ability to process information.

This happens because the workings of the body, mind, and spirit are inextricably bound up in one another. When any one of these is negatively affected, the entire system quickly becomes out of balance.

For this reason, it's important to understand the dangers of not having a harmonious mind, body, and spirit connection. The mind-body-spirit connection can lead to physical ailments, depending on the mental choices we make. In order for the body to remain healthy and energized, there must be a balance among all three, because the body responds to our thoughts, feelings, and actions.

In this chapter, I'll briefly cover important information about how the body, mind, and spirit work together, as well as healing modalities that work especially well for treating problems with each of these components that make up our unique and beautiful selves. For more information on any of these topics, please visit my website at www.journeystoheal.com.

Understanding the Physical Body

The body is incredibly sensitive to what is going on with each one of us on all levels—mentally, emotionally, and spiritually.

When you choose to live with the toxins of stress, anxiety, un-forgiveness, fear, and anger for long periods of time, that toxic energy eventually becomes stagnant. The stagnant energy stores itself in certain areas of the body, resulting in a variety of physical ailments, as well as a weakened immune system, making us more likely to get colds and other infections during emotionally difficult times.

When a physical ailment is manifested in the body, this is simply the body's way of telling us that our energy is out of balance. The easiest way to help yourself understand where these negative emotions are stored and what their message is, is to pay attention to where you are experiencing a physical issue in the body.

Learning about the chakras and the importance of each one's role in our physical, mental, emotional, and spiritual bodies can be of great help in pinpointing the real message about what is wrong that underlies these signals from your body. More information about the chakras, including what they are, how they work, and how to work with them to stimulate healing, is available to you at my website, www.journeystoheal.com.

In addition to working with your chakras, there are many solutions and healing modalities that can be useful in treating and healing physical issues in the body. In the following sections, I briefly discuss several of these. The information given here is intended only to give a brief overview of what each solution is and how it can be used to promote your own healing. Consider each of these as another stepping stone on the path to mental and physical wellness.

Food Intake

What we eat, when we eat it, and how much food we place into our bodies determines how much energy we will have to function and how clear our minds will be. Vegetables and fruits grown in the earth carry high-frequency energy, so when you intro-duce these high-energy foods into your body, you automatically increase your body's frequency and your energy remains high. This can help you stay clear of colds and other common illnesses.

Healthy food habits, such as introducing greens and vege-tables, not allowing the body to feel starved, and eating small, healthy portions five times per day, will allow your mind to remain at a balance. Juicing fresh fruits and vegetables is another good option to accommodate a busy lifestyle that does not always allow room to meet your body's daily nutrition requirements.

Water Intake

When I first started my spiritual journey, one of the most profound teachings I received was the importance of water intake. Water intake helps maintain the balance of fluid in the body, which controls calories, energizes the muscles, and keeps the skin looking healthy, young, and fresh. Most importantly, it cleanses the kidneys and helps maintain normal bowel function. Remember, more than 70 percent of our bodies and the Earth is water. We use water to cleanse our bodies externally; it is equally important to drink six to eight glasses of water a day to cleanse our bodies internally.

It is also very important where and how you store your water. Drinking water from a glass or pure copper bottle has many health benefits. Copper charged water for 8-10 hours kills harmful bacteria and when the copper reacts with the water, it becomes ionized, maintaining the body's pH balance. Writing positive words on your glass bottle such as: love, health, peace, happiness is another way to charge your water.

The Power of Play for Adults and Children

Spiritually speaking, play time for children *and* adults is crucial. At all ages and stages of life, play time allows our minds, bodies, and spirits to experience joy and laughter. For this reason, play time is vital for problem solving, creativity, and the survival of our relationships.

Stuart Brown, MD, author, psychiatrist, and founder of the National Institute for Play, believes play consists of art, books, movies, music, comedy, flirting, and daydreaming. He says play is like oxygen; we cannot survive or thrive without it. Play also has the power to lead us to a sacred space, cultivating healing within us and spreading it to others around us.

Integrated Energy Therapy® (IET)

Developed by Stevan J. Thayer in 1994, Integrated Energy Therapy® (IET) is a powerful, hands-on energy healing modality that removes emotional issues or obstacles on a cellular level. It utilizes violet angelic energy rays, supporting you to safely and gently release the limiting energy patterns from your past and empowering your life in the present.

IET therapy focuses on specific meridian points that have the power to support the clearing of energy blocks from the body. These energy blockages are the result of deeply suppressed cellular memory that are often the result of dis-ease, trauma, surgery, stress, fears, self-limiting thoughts, and other negative illusions that affect the mind and body. When all these negative blockages are released, the individual experiences healing in all areas of his or her life.

The Benefits of Reiki

The word *Reiki* is Japanese for universal life-force energy. It is an ancient laying-on-of-hands healing technique that transfers life-force energy into the body. This accelerates the body's natural healing process, making Reiki effective for pain, muscle spasms, stress, and fatigue. It also helps release emotional blockages, stimulates the immune system, and is especially effective for chronic and acute illnesses, such as cancer.

Although Reiki is a wonderful energy healing modality, offering many benefits to cancer patients and others in need, it is not a substitute for traditional medical treatments. Still, it is a safe and highly effective technique for reducing side effects and speeding up the recovery process when utilized in conjunction with other medical and therapeutic systems.

The Benefits of Emotional Freedom Technique

Discovered by Dr. Roger Callahan in the 1980s, Emotional Freedom Technique (EFT; also commonly called "tapping") is a simple yet highly effective technique that can be learned by anyone. This healing modality works with the body's energy system, or chi, which is carried through the meridian pathways—some of the same points used in acupressure and acupuncture.

Essentially, EFT is a method where the fingertips are used to tap at the face and upper body's various energy meridians, while one is tuned in to the issue that needs to be healed. This process balances the energy interruption that continually triggers the negative thought or behavior, getting to the core of the issue and releasing it. EFT has been successfully used to treat weight loss, allergies, fears, anxiety, sadness, pain, anger, phobias, negative beliefs, headaches, stress, chronic fatigue, low self-esteem, and many other illusions perceived by the mind.

Understanding the Mind

In order to live in a constant state of love and peace, it is important to understand how the mind works. The mind consists of the left hemisphere (left brain) and the right hemisphere (right brain). The left brain is responsible for our logic and ego, while the right brain is home to our creativity and connection to Source.

In addition to these two hemispheres, the mind is further separated into the conscious and subconscious. The conscious mind consists of your logic, reason, intelligence, and willpower and takes up about 12 percent of your brain power. Like a hard drive, the subconscious mind takes up 88 percent of your brain power, containing every negative and positive behavior and experience from your past.

The way that the subconscious mind works is bittersweet. Because it does not discriminate between reality and fiction, whatever you feed it is what it perceives to be real. For this reason, the subconscious mind has the power to change old behaviors and create new ones within twenty-one to thirty days. If we are faced with an experience for at least this long, it becomes a part of our new behavior or belief system regardless of its energy—whether positive or negative.

It may be that you consciously desire to release obstacles. However, if your subconscious behavior dictates otherwise, this change will not come to pass. Because our willpower exists on a conscious level, overcoming negative behaviors or beliefs rooted in the subconscious can be very difficult. The good news is that it can be done. Below, I highlight some simple yet powerful tools, modalities, and lifestyle changes that, when applied, have the power to help you achieve any positive change you desire.

Through the power of your mind's energy, you too can live in a constant state of grace through choice.

Benefits of Daily Journaling

Journaling offers many benefits. Some of these are that it evokes mindfulness, increases the memory, and creates happiness from the inside out.

I often assign clients the exercise of journaling the negative events from their day or their past on loose sheets of paper. They are instructed to safely burn these pages or throw them away after writing these thoughts down, burning away the illusions and frustrations of the past as well as anxieties about the future. This process helps the individual to process his or her emotions and develop greater self-awareness. After this process is complete, they can then end the day by writing in their gratitude journals, focusing on all the experiences they are grateful for in the past, present, and future—writing it all down in the present tense.

By actively engaging with your goals in the present tense, you increase the likelihood of achieving them by signaling to your brain that this information is important. Just like a muscle, the more you exercise the power of your mind, the stronger it becomes. Likewise, the more baggage you release, the more you clear your internal closet.

Journaling leads to mental, emotional, and physical healing, clearing away the clutter caused by trauma from the past. Studies show journaling lowers anxiety and stress, and induces better sleep. It also helps us to get back in touch with our own creativity. Free-flow journaling awakens our deeper creative selves, bringing to the surface thoughts and ideas we may not have believed we had in us.

Most importantly, gratitude journaling allows your brain to relive positive feelings and experiences. This reinforces your gifts and talents, releasing dopamine and endorphins (chemicals associated with feeling happy) in the brain, thereby boosting your mood and self-confidence. With patience and consistency, you too can form this simple yet powerful new habit that will change your life.

The Benefits of Hypnotherapy

A proven therapeutic process, hypnotherapy is one of the most natural and effective ways to help you overcome physical, mental, emotional, and even spiritual obstacles and improve the quality of your life. This is a healing modality whereby suggestion is used to guide your imagination toward a relaxed and focused state. Then, via guided visualization, mental pictures (such as images of positive healing) combined with hypnotic suggestion are utilized to restore inner peace and create the framework for emotional, spiritual, and physical healing.

Because the act of conjuring imagery is rooted in the underlying idea that the body and mind are interconnected, this practice allows participants to use their own senses to heal both the body and the mind. In hypnotherapy, positive imagery is used for relaxation and to lower blood pressure, reduce stress, reach goals, manage pain, and promote overall healing. In addition to promoting healing, this relaxed state encourages improved learning, creativity, and performance. It helps you feel more in control of your emotions and thought processes.

The therapeutic imagery of hypnotherapy is safe and is often combined with conventional medical treatment to facilitate healing.

The Healing Practice of Meditation

A truly ancient technique for balancing the mind, body, and spirit, meditation was originally meant to help deepen our understanding of the sacred and mystical forces of life. Today, we meditate not only to connect with Source, but also to achieve relaxation and to heal from mental, emotional, and physical obstacles.

When you meditate, you clear away the information overload and mental chatter that builds up in the brain and contributes to stress. The benefits of this effect are endless. Due to its immense value, it's no surprise that meditation has been in practice for thousands of years. Individuals who meditate regularly live happier and healthier lives with reduced stress and, in some cases, experience a reversal of many forms of dis-ease.

There are over 23 forms of meditation, such as yoga, qigong, tai chi, mindfulness, loving kindness, mantra meditation, and more. Personally, I love and deeply connect with guided meditation, which allows you to create helpful imagery and visualize your goals and dreams. I also love meditations that use the repetition of mantras. If you're interested in learning more about meditation, please visit my website at www.journeystoheal.com for access to guided meditation CD's and mantras that have helped my clients live happier, healthier, and more stress-free lives.

The Benefits of Sleep for Adults and Children

Sleep is essential for our mental, emotional, and physical health, because our sleeping habits dictate how our minds—and thus, our thoughts and bodies—function. Millions of people around the world either suffer from lack of sleep or simply don't get enough of it. I know this all too well, because nearly all of my clients—both adults and children—have this issue when they come to me for healing.

When we fail to get a full night's sleep, the mind misses out on its chance to vent and release the mental clutter it picks up throughout the day. The result is an overloaded brain, leading to increased mind chatter. Each night when we go to bed and experience the sleep state, this gives the mind a chance to vent unimportant events and information and to relax, rejuvenate, and recharge itself. Then we can wake up feeling rested, energized, and clear minded. On average, eight hours of peaceful, restful, uninterrupted sleep per night is required to achieve this state.

The Effects of Television

We often forget the importance of creating peace in the mind. Negative lifestyle choices force us into stress, anxiety, panic attacks, and depression, but by making simple shifts and changes in our lives, we can help restore our peace. One of the simplest changes is paying attention to what we watch on television and when we watch it. To keep the mind free from extra external negative downloads, we should steer away from watching negative television such as drama, horror, or the news early in the morning or late at night, before bedtime.

The subconscious mind is in its most suggestible state at least two hours prior to bedtime and for at least half an hour after we wake up in the morning, so your subconscious, like a sponge, absorbs anything you introduce to the mind at those times, and that information becomes the driving force of your day, week, month, and year, depending on how long you introduce that same negative information. The simplest remedy for this issue is to either not watch television late at night and early in the morning or, if you have to, simply focus on making positive choices to watch comedy or programs that lift you up and help you feel good.

Understanding the Spirit

No matter what culture, race, or religious background we come from, we have all heard our loved ones say that prayer helps us heal. Prayer is like having a special phone line to connect with Source, to go within, and we all have that number. It is one of the most simple and yet powerful ways to reconnect with the universe and with our higher selves.

Much research and many personal testimonies exist on the power of positive intent and prayer. One of the most profound pieces of research in this field was performed by Dr. Masaru Emoto. He found that the power of our intent or prayer can physically affect water crystals—either positively or negatively. When people pray over water, its crystals form beautiful snow-flake-like patterns, thus becoming healing water. Consider that the human body is made up of more than 70 percent water. Now imagine what the power of positive prayer can do for our bodies.

That said, it's important to know how to pray in a positive manner. I have seen hundreds of clients come my way with the same frustration: they had prayed on something, and they felt that their prayer was not answered. After seeing several cases of this, I became curious and started to ask how my clients were praying. What I heard from them was shocking. Each person who had prayed and was still living a life filled with turmoil, grief, and sorrow was simply praying the wrong way.

For instance, one of my female clients came to me in tears, because her family was falling apart. When I asked her if she had been praying, she said, "Of course. I pray every day." I asked her to give me an example of one of her prayers, and she replied, "Well, I ask God not to break up my family, and for us not to get sick." There was her problem, plain and simple.

You have already learned in previous chapters that what we think, focus on, and feel is what we manifest into our reality. Because the universe is extremely literal, it does not discriminate between your negative and positive words and energy. It simply provides what you ask for. For this reason, there are two important things to do when you offer up a prayer. First, you must pray with wholehearted belief that the universe heard your prayer and has already granted it. Second, and most importantly, you must use *only positive words* in your prayer. Remember, intention is everything.

My client whose family was falling apart needed only to use different, positive words to make her intent more clear to the universe. In order to see the response she was seeking, she needed to say instead, "I choose health and healing. I choose love. And I ask that you bring health into my loved ones' bodies."

With positive prayer and intent, you will notice that your intuition will improve as well. Thus, when you pray, you will know deep in your heart and soul that the prayer has been received and the answer given.

In addition to the power of positive prayer, the following solutions will help you to find the peace and balance your spirit needs to help further aid you in your quest for healing.

The Benefit of Intuition

Intuition is the divine voice, the inner voice inside of us, and it speaks to us always. It does this in the form of the hunches you get—inner knowing, visions, or gut feelings that come freely, without the need for conscious reasoning. It is very easy to dismiss this inner voice, because most of us are overwhelmed with the ego chatter, but if you allow yourself to listen to it, it is a great gift. The power of intuition allows you to make decisions that lead to greatness, because you are connected to your inner wisdom.

We are all born intuitive because we are spirits having a human experience. When we are young, our consciousness or intuition is highly alert, and we listen to and follow this voice. But as we grow, our ego mind is formed, and we tend to adopt the beliefs of our loved ones and friends. This shift forces us to forget and move away from our natural intuition.

Paying attention and trusting your intuition is one of the most powerful tools available to you that will allow you to reconnect with your authentic self. Meditation is one of the tools that reconnect us to that inner voice of truth. The next time you predict a future event before it happens, you will know you are tapped into your intuition. One of the best ways to reconnect with this inner wisdom is to journal your intuitive insights. The more that you trust this inner sense, the more powerful it will become.

The Power of Intention

Intention is the first step on our spiritual journey to higher consciousness. Think of it as a tiny seed you send out into the universe to allow it to take root in the physical world. Once it blossoms, it will bring you the fruit of your desires made manifest. When you set an intention to obtain or find your true self, your entire life shifts. Every experience becomes a catalyst that brings you closer to who you truly are, and to a place of love and acceptance.

The trick here is not just to "want" things. Remember, the universe is literal. So when we continually focus on the energy of wanting, we are focusing on lack. In turn, when we *want* to be successful, happy, or loved, we are actually chasing the lack of these things. But by turning our wants into the *intention* to be happy, successful, loved, and prosperous, we intensify the spark of that wonderfully unforgettable feeling inside our hearts and draw all the wonder that life holds toward us.

When you live rooted in intention, you approach life with the optimism that miracles and gifts are arriving in your life all the time. Infinite creativity lives at the realm of universal consciousness, and you can tap into this through your positive intentions.

The Power of Gratitude

Perhaps most importantly, live your daily life through gratitude. Expressing gratitude in our daily lives is the bond that holds humanity together, and it is essential for our survival. Because the universe is literal, and because the thoughts and emotions we send out determine our experiences, gratitude is uniquely powerful. Your gratitude is a direct message to the universe that says, "I choose more of this." That message triggers a steady flow of the blessings for which you are grateful—creating a powerful positive feedback loop.

For this reason, the key to continuous fulfillment and joy is living in a state of perpetual gratitude rather than taking the blessings in our lives for granted. The daily practice of living in gratitude will help keep your heart open to attract positive experiences, regardless of whatever challenges you may be facing at the time.

The Secret to a Successful Life

Once you understand how intrinsically the body, mind, and spirit are linked to one another, the secret to a successful and fulfilled life is simple. Every decision we make determines the level of our physical, mental, and emotional happiness. Too often, we equate success with the constant greed for obtaining more material goods. But the truth is that we cannot enjoy life if we experience constant fear of lack, of losing what we have, or greed to obtain more.

The presence of this illusion—that to obtain more material for the future is the definition of success—leads to a false sense of security. We must awaken to the truth that safety and security come only from within—from Source. No material object in the world has the capacity to guarantee our safety or security. The material things we experience in life provide only temporary gratification. When your inner spiritual world is fulfilled, peaceful, and filled with love, your outer material world will automatically match it.

This is the Law of Attraction at work; what you think and feel inside manifests and shows up in your outer world and experiences.

Being able to live life in the present moment means practicing patience and living in gratitude for all your experiences. This is what leads us to enlightenment. Chasing material goods or greed takes us away from ourselves, our loved ones, and the divine, which is truly the only source that provides eternal abundance. When we fail to be present and enjoy the moment with our loved ones, we are not practicing inner peace or spiritual success.

A life of peace, positivity, and patience, however, offers unlimited dividends. In the next and final chapter, I will show you how regular spiritual practice and reconnection with Source, the inner self, can bring you the health, happiness, and prosperity you dream of enjoying. You'll also learn how you can direct the light inside yourself outward, shining it like a beacon into the world to bring others around you to a place of spiritual balance, joy, love, and peace.

Chapter 11

The Journey Comes Full Circle

I slept and dreamt that life was joy. I woke and saw that life was service. I acted and behold service was joy.

—*Rabindranath Tagore*

"Healer, Heal Yourself"

Jesus wisely said, "Love your neighbor as you love yourself." But it's important to remember that, in the absence of one, the other cannot exist. We must remember to first be of service to ourselves before we can effectively be of service to others.

Being good stewards of ourselves starts with taking a long, hard look at what we think we know about wellness. Our society has been programmed to look for quick fixes when it comes to love, health, happiness, success, and family. But we tend to forget that these quick fixes cannot lead to permanent positive results—not when they treat only our symptoms, rather than the underlying root of the problems we experience.

No matter what challenges we face, the key to permanent health and happiness lies in spirituality, self-love, and the release of fears, anger, unforgiveness, and other toxic emotions.

We must also constantly remind ourselves that embodying

either negativity or positivity is a choice. We make this choice day to day, and minute to minute. Whichever path you choose will determine your experiences.

As we've learned, the source of the negativity that we experience is the ego mind. Operating from the ego mind only strengthens the illusion of fear that keeps us trapped in negativity, because the ego's job is to separate you from your authentic self. This state of living in fear is, in essence, the total opposite of embodying your spiritual truth: a state of awareness of our eternal connection to the divine and unending love.

The intent to live spiritually and be positive opens the door to live and experience heaven on earth. By reconnecting to your heart—the conduit to love, joy, happiness, and prosperity—you reconnect to your divinity. And by mindfully practicing simple acts of kindness, such as smiling and offering help to those in need, you not only exercise self-love and love for others, but also tap into the powerful universal energy to attract positive situations, opportunities, and people to yourself.

This selfless practice leads to a fulfilled life—not just for you, but also for those around you.

Heal Yourself, Heal the World

All around the world, millions of people suffer from the negative effects of stress, anger, addictions, and depression due to the limiting beliefs instilled in them by friends and family. The evidence of this is manifested on the daily news and in the tragic stories we hear from our surrounding neighborhoods: adults and children using illegal drugs and killing themselves and others, and the current epidemic of addiction to prescription drugs.

For too long, we have allowed ourselves to remain oblivious to the fact that we are all spiritual beings of pure energy. When one hurts, we all hurt. That's because our energy has the power to affect thousands of people all around us. When we are miserable, we spread that toxic energy into everyone and everything that surrounds us—and even into the natural world. But the reverse is equally true; when we experience joy and love, we send out positive, healing energy toward everything and everyone who crosses our paths.

When we dwell in the energy of love, our minds and bodies are positively affected. The heart expands when we experience the energy of love. Our minds release chemicals such as dopamine, adrenaline, and norepinephrine, lighting up the brain's pleasure center. Imagine if the entire world operated on the energy of love: there would be no wars, no hurting or killing one another. Peace and happiness would truly rule the world.

We all have the power within us to shift the collective energy of humanity to this higher state of spiritual awareness and joy. By choosing to experience positive energy and being of service to others, we free ourselves from the toxic energy that traps us in illusions of fear and dis-ease. We create a collective homeostasis within ourselves and everyone else around us, activating the miracle of healing around the world. This powerful collective shift is experienced around the world during the holidays, when everyone is filled with the joy of giving and receiving.

A Guide to Walk beside You

Your experiences make up the steps along the path of your unique journey. Combined with the tools in this book, this journey can become a catalyst to lead you to your own spiritual truth and enlightenment. I invite you to experiment with any of the tools I have introduced you to in these pages. At the same time, remember to honor your mind, body, and spirit by choosing only those exercises that speak to you.

I also invite you to use your creativity and imagination, and let your intuition guide your journey to spiritual wholeness. Remember not to force or expect results, but rather work through each step of your healing with an open mind. Trust and believe that the healing techniques that speak to you will be effective.

If you'd like to learn more about any of the topics I've covered, you will find the resources you need to continue your spiritual journey on my website (www.journeystoheal.com). There, I offer supplemental materials including guided meditation CD's, mantras and affirmations, and more in-depth information on some of the health topics and healing modalities I've introduced you to here.

You can also find information on upcoming workshops, retreats, and classes and connect with me in person. I realized from a very young age that my purpose in this lifetime is to be of service, by acting as a guide on your journey to healing. I am honored to embody this role as a vessel and teacher for those of you who seek me out, and I would love to hear from you. I invite you to share your healing stories with me by sending me an email at kristine@journeystoheal.com.

The Next Step in Your Journey to Wholeness

Since my own surrender to my higher self and the healing I have received in my own life, I have had the blessing of helping thousands of others like me find and reconnect to their paths to live as their authentic selves.

Some of you reading this book may be recovering from cancer or other illnesses, while others may be feeling lost or helpless against the many physical, mental, or emotional illusions I've described in these pages. Or maybe you are reading this book simply because it interested you.

In any case, this book, and the wisdom it contains, is not intended only for those in crisis, but for all beautiful souls who are curious and searching for simple yet powerful tools to help them realize their own spiritual power and transformation.

My clients and I are living proof, that by changing your thoughts and behaviors, you will change your life. As you set your intentions to advance along your spiritual path, not only will you positively affect your own life, but you will become a powerful catalyst for healing change in the lives of those around you. You will tap into the energy of universal truth and experience more love, peace, joy, and abundance, which will expand from your heart into your energy and auric fields and out into everything around you.

With dedication, soon you will notice that living a spiritually fulfilled life becomes your lifestyle, just like eating and sleeping. Once you tap into that energy, the rewards are endless. The more you dive into this energy and information by joining groups or talking to others who share your new knowledge and wisdom, the more you will expand and grow.

Celebrate and be in gratitude for your miraculous existence, and remember that your mind, body, and spirit are more than just a physical construct. Your body is not just flesh and bones; it is the awe-inspiring assembly of organ systems whose synchronized functioning is a miracle of its own.

Tapping into your spiritual self will lead you to an existence filled with joy, love, clarity, peace, and overall fulfillment in all areas of your life. You hold the power to create love and peace in the world by shifting your consciousness and the consciousness of the people around you. All that is needed to claim this power is to set out on this journey of spiritual surrender that I have invited you to take part in.

In the pages of this book, I've given you the tools you need to equip yourself to handle obstacles that present themselves in your path along the way. Now it's up to you to take the next step.

I put so much of my heart and love into this book that I wholeheartedly believe that every beautiful soul who holds it in his or her hands will tap into the powerful healing benefits of the divine.

I wish you all the best that life can offer. Know that each day when you love, I love with you. When you smile, I smile with you.

Each and every day, choose to be a conscious creator. Live through choice and create what you truly desire through the power of your thoughts, and watch miracles unfold and exceed your expectations.

May love and light shine on all your dreams.

REFERENCES

Bourne, E. J. (2001). *The anxiety and phobia workbook: A step-by-step program for curing yourself of extreme anxiety, panic attacks, and phobias.* New York, NY: MJF Books.

Brainwave Research Institute. (n.d.). *Meditation increases serotonin levels.* Retrieved from http://brainwave-research-institute.com/meditation-increases-serotonin-levels-.html

Brussat, F., & Brussat, M. A. (n.d.). Practicing patience: Specific ways to practice the counter-cultural stance of patience in daily life, with a group, in your relationships, and with God. *Spirituality & Practice: Resources for Spiritual Journeys.* Retrieved from http://www.spiritualityandpractice.com/practices/features.php?id=18801

Depression. (2015). In *A View on Buddhism.* Retrieved from http://viewonbuddhism.org/depression.html

Guided imagery. (2008). *Mayo Clinic Health Letter, 26*(1), 6.

Hudacek, K. (2007). A review of the effects of hypnosis on the immune system in breast cancer patients: Brief communication. *The International Journal of Clinical and Experimental Hypnosis, 55*(4), 411–425.

Jesus, C., & Morgan, J. C. (1990). *Jesus and mastership: The gospel according to Jesus of Nazareth as dictated through James Coyle Morgan.* Tacoma, WA: Oakbridge University Press.

Juliani, A. (2006). *Reiki: The Usui system of natural healing, level 1 manual*. Los Angeles, CA: American Reiki Academy.

Kappas, S. (2009). *Advanced EFT: Emotional freedom technique – Parts 1 and 2: Finding peace, joy, and freedom*. www.susiekappas.com

Kouwe, K. (n.d.). Biofrequency and disease. *Embracelight.com*. Retrieved from http://www.embracelight.com/ylessentialoils/essentialoilfrequencies.html

Lengacher, C. A., Bennett, M. P., Gonzalez, L., Gilvary, D., Cox, C. E., & Cantor, A. (2008). Immune responses to guided imagery during breast cancer treatment. *Biological Research for Nursing, 9*(3), 205–214.

León-Pizarro, C., Gich, I., Barthe, E., Rovirosa, A., Farrús, B., Casas, F., . . . Arcusa, A. (2007). A randomized trial of the effect of training in relaxation and guided imagery techniques in improving psychological and quality-of-life indices for gynecologic and breast brachytherapy patients. *Psycho-Oncology, 16*(11), 971–979.

Mayo Clinic Staff. (2011). Stress management. *Mayo Clinic*. Retrieved from http://www.mayoclinic.com/health/stress-management/MY00435

Miles, P. (2007). Reiki for mind, body and spirit support of cancer patients. *Advances, 22*(2), 20–26. Retrieved from http://advancesjournal.com/pdfarticles/miles.pdf

Ovsepian, K. (2013). *Journeys to heal*. Retrieved from www.journeystoheal.com

Pedersen, T. (2014). How spirituality protects the brain

against depression. *Psych Central.* Retrieved from http://psychcentral.com/news/2014/01/19/how-spirituality-protects-the-brain-against-depression/64698.html

Potter, P. J. (2007). Breast biopsy and distress: Feasibility of testing a Reiki intervention. *Journal of Holistic Nursing, 25*(4), 238–248.

Rossman, M. L. (2004). Guided imagery in cancer care. *Seminars in Integrative Medicine, 2*(3), 99–106.

Seda, L. (2013, January 10). 10 warning signs you're addicted to suffering. *The Change Blog.* Retrieved from http://www.thechangeblog.com/addicted-to-suffering/

Tartakovsky, M. (2012). The importance of play for adults. *Psych Central.* Retrieved from http://psychcentral.com/blog/archives/2012/11/15/the-importance-of-play-for-adults/

Thayer, S. J. (1994–2010). *Integrated energy therapy: Basic to advanced level guides.* Woodstock, NY: The Center of Being.

Turner-Schott, C. (2009). Neptune: Alcoholism, addictions & spiritual awakening. *SelfGrowth.com.* Retrieved from http://www.selfgrowth.com/articles/neptune_alcoholism_addictions_spiritual_awakening

WebMD. (2016). What is depression? *Depression Health Center.* Retrieved from http://www.webmd.com/depression/guide/what-is-depression?page=3

Zelman, K. M. (2008). 6 reasons to drink water. *WebMD.* Retrieved from http://www.webmd.com/diet/features/6-reasons-to-drink-water

LIST OF RECOMMENDED BOOKS

The Power of Now: A Guide to Spiritual Enlightenment by Eckhart Tolle

Ask and It Is Given by Esther and Jerry Hicks

Mirrors of Time by Brian L. Weiss, MD

Many Lives, Many Masters by Brian L. Weiss, MD

Same Soul, Many Bodies by Brian L. Weiss, MD

The Reconnection by Dr. Eric Pearl

Trust in God: The Miracle of Healing by Gloria Gardner

To Heaven and Back by Mary C. Neal, MD

Jeshua the Personal Christ Volumes I, II, III by Judith Coates and Alan Cohen

Constant Craving by Doreen Virtue

Jesus and Mastership: The Gospel According to Jesus of Nazareth as dictated through James Coyle Morgan

The Silva Mind Control Method by José Silva

Conversations with God by Neale Donald Walsch

Infinite Self: 33 Steps to Reclaiming Your Inner Power by Stuwart Wilde

Wishes Fulfilled by Wayne W. Dyer

A Return to Love by Marianne Williamson

LIST OF RECOMMENDED
DOCUMENTARIES

The Secret
3 Magic Words
What the Bleep Do We Know?
2012: An Awakening
2012: Time for Change
2012: Mayan Prophecy
Happy
Afterlife
Fat, Sick and Nearly Dead
Forks over Knifes
Vegucated
Food Matters
The Beautiful Truth
The Gerson Miracle
Dying to Have Known
DMT: The Spirit Molecule
The Flowering of Human Consciousness
Be Still
Hungry for Change
Stress: Portrait of a Killer
10 Questions for the Dalai Lama
Wake Up

ABOUT THE AUTHOR

Kristine Ovsepian, MA, C.Ht, is the owner and founder of Journeys to Heal and Journeys to Heal Retreats LLC. As a gifted spiritual counselor, energy healer, life coach, and hypnotherapist, Kristine works in her private practice in the Los Angeles area and takes groups on spiritual retreats around the world. Because Kristine has an extensive background in psychology and ancient healing modalities, she works with each client according to his or her own belief system. Thus, every session with Kristine is unique, powerful, and healing.

Kristine believes being present in each moment frees us from the burdens of the past and future. She helps her clients awaken to the amazing potential of healing by releasing burdens in all areas of their lives, in order to live each moment to the fullest. Kristine continues to facilitate the healing of thousands of clients, assisting them to take decisive action and transform their lives. Kristine lives in the Los Angeles area with her husband, two children, and dog Coco.